CELEBRITIES in Hiding

by Audrey Moe

Also written and illustrated
by Audrey Schumacher Moe

Beachwalk
An Everyday Journey Through Sea, Sand and Soul

Desertwalk
A Search For Secrets of the Desert

Celebrities in Hiding

by Audrey Moe

Hiding

Published byWalk Publishing, LLC
14505 Yerxa Road
Desert Hot Springs, CA 92240

Celebrities in Hiding
ISBN 9780974988535
Library of Congress Control Number 2012937990

For purchase information please contact:
cih@walkpublishing.com

Cover Design & Book Layout
Orlando Ramos | orlando@DonGatoGraphics.com

Preface

Celebrities In Hiding came about almost by accident. Through casual conversations with a few long time desert residents, small anecdotes involving celebrities began to pop up. I realized if they were not preserved, soon they would be lost forever.

The stories are told in the words of those who experienced them and in some cases, where details of remembrance are sketchy, the experience is related as it could have happened.

The celebrity sightings took place during a time span of seventy-five years, begining in the 1930's and involved a geographical area ten miles north of Palm Springs. Details fleshing out celebrity profiles enrich each chapter and references to historical events serve to ground the stories in time.

My gratitude goes to those people who were willing to relate their experiences or who gave me leads to follow. They are all acknowledged at the end of the book. Were it not for these contacts, historical and revealing insights involving celebrity visitors would be lost like grains of sand scattered in the desert winds.

Chapter List

Introduction

Celebrity watching has never been a hobby of mine. Oh, sure, I've had my moments. When I lived in Newport Beach, I once stood in line at the Balboa Island post office with Buddy Ebsen from the *Beverly Hillbillies.* I felt a small stab of excitement to be that close to someone I'd become so familiar with on the TV screen.

And, yes, I'd craned my neck to see if it was truly John Wayne in the group gathered on the dock of his home on Newport Bay as my husband and I sailed past on our Hobie catamaran one Sunday afternoon.

When a friend pointed out Joseph Waumbaugh's elegant copper-trimmed home on Newport Coast, I felt a vague wave of interest, but not enough to make it worth jotting down the address.

Tennis fans sometimes reminded me we'd purchased our home in tennis star, Rod Laver's, old neighborhood. But it took several reminders before I actually remembered that piece of information and made it my own.

Honestly, I simply didn't care enough about the lives of the famous to be more than casually interested. Catching a small glimpse or hearing a bit of news about a well-known personality just didn't seem to be anything I was interested in.

When we moved away from the Newport Beach community on the California coast and settled in a small, sleepy, desert town north of Palm Springs, I assumed any casual celebrity sightings were over. Palm Springs was a celebrity magnet, but not Desert Hot Springs where we lived. That is until one evening at dinner in the picturesque dining room of Two Bunch Palms Spa and Resort.

As my husband and I, along with another couple, sat at our table for four, chatting and catching up on times past, our friend to my right, nudged me gently with his elbow and said, "Don't look now, but guess who's sitting at the table next to us?"

Of course, with my curiosity aroused, I immediately glanced to my left at the tiny table for two nestled against the wall. I found myself looking directly at Barbra Streisand who was conversing animatedly with a gentleman whom I did not recognize. I quickly turned back to our table, feeling guilty for having stared.

I was aware that Two Bunch Palms fiercely guards its guests from public scrutiny. Several months earlier on a tour with the manager, we had been instructed to never approach, speak to, stare at or ask any celebrity for an autograph. At the time, the warnings seemed almost ludicrous, but now I understood the need for being forewarned.

When we left the dining room that evening after lingering over dessert and coffee, I managed one more tiny sideways peek at Streisand. Then I pushed my chair out and passed within a few feet of her, still pretending I didn't even notice. The incident impressed our out-of-town friends and we talked about it in the car driving back to our house. "Where else," I said, "could she have had dinner out and remained totally undisturbed?"

Several years later on a Sunday morning while having breakfast at the Sidewinder, a restaurant frequented by locals in Desert Hot Springs, and one which has remained unchanged for over forty years, who should walk in but Martha Stewart accompanied by three young people. They were seated in a corner booth and the restaurant owner, with obvious pleasure, served them herself. This was after Stewart had served her jail sentence for lying about a stock transaction and had returned to running her TV show and magazine, *Martha Stewart Living.* So here was another celebrity in a totally unexpected place.

After that sighting, I couldn't help but wonder why celebrities would appear in this small desert town as far away as I could imagine from where I thought famous people might be attracted.

Upscale restaurants, elite homes and expensive boutiques simply did not exist in Desert Hot Springs. When I dug into the issue, I realized the attraction is precisely because it "is" an unlikely place for celebrities and therefore it serves as a hideaway for those seeking privacy. The thought, newly planted in my mind, sat like a seed in the ground waiting for the right circumstances to cause it to sprout.

Once I began focusing on celebrities who had been seen in Desert Hot Springs, stories about movie stars and famous people exploded like popcorn in a microwave: Marilyn Monroe, Gary Cooper, Jennifer Jones, John Travolta, Frank Sinatra, Mamie Eisenhower. An endless cavalcade of well-known personalities emerged along with those whom I wouldn't recognize in person, like the director, Robert Altman, whose name and innovative movie work are celebrated world wide.

As long time Desert Hot Springs residents learned I was interested in their celebrity experiences, they began sharing stories from as far back as the 1940's when popular dude ranches in Seven Palms Valley (an early name for the Desert Hot Springs area) drew the Hollywood elite as well as business and industrial giants. In these interviews, fresh and fascinating anecdotes surfaced. Glimpses into the true character of a celebrity became a common theme throughout. Woven into their stories are threads of the history and spirit of the times.

During this period when possibilities were endless and dreams complemented reality, tales of people and history patched together in a quilt of desert living provide a colorful picture. These are the never before told stories in *Celebrities In Hiding*.

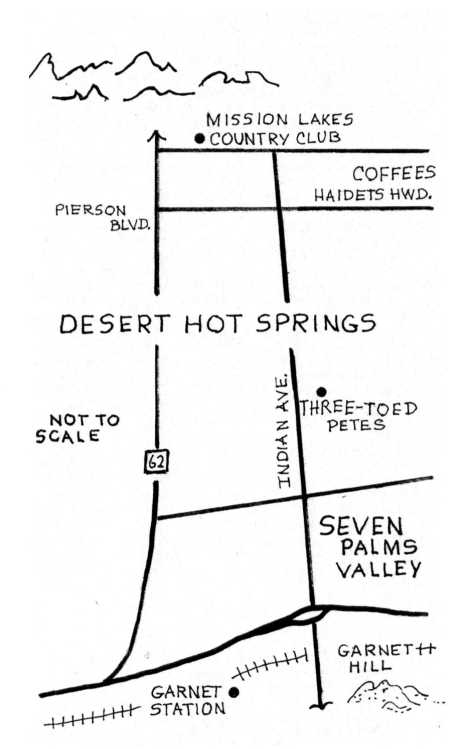

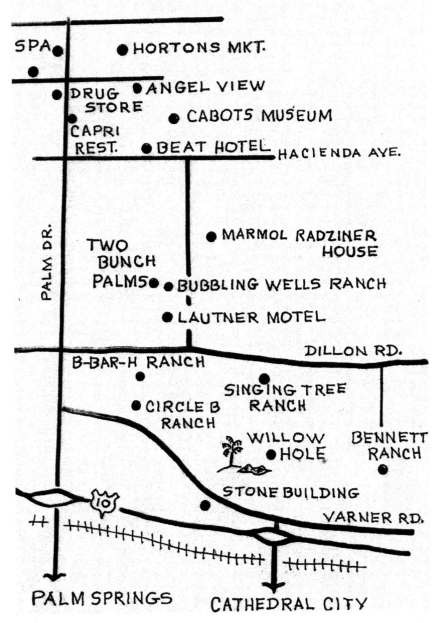

STALKERS, THREATS AND ATTEMPTED ABDUCTION
Janet Gaynor

Careers that lead to fame may seem glamorous and desirable, but they also have drawbacks. Janet Gaynor, a huge star during the silent movie era, was one of those celebrities who was threatened by too much adoration from some of her fans.

The first letter came from Kalamazoo, Michigan. Janet, at her desert retreat, was not too concerned. Michigan was a long way from Seven Palms Valley, a remote swath of alluvial plain slanting downward from the Little San Bernardino Mountains to the desert floor of the Coachella Valley. Still, it was unpleasant to read the words of a strange man who said he was in love with her and was coming to get her. He threatened to take her away with him, away from Adrian, her husband, who he said didn't deserve her. Janet shrugged off the creepy feeling his words had on her and tossed the letter into the waste basket.

She felt safe with Adrian, an MGM costume designer well known and respected in the movie industry. His last name was Golden, though he seldom used it and asked to be referred to by his first name only. Together they sought privacy and a place to get away from the frantic world of movie making. Their rustic cabin in Seven Palms Valley, known today as Desert Hot Springs was surrounded by desert dunes, creosote bushes, small washes, and stands of smoke trees and tamarisk. It suited them well.

Janet was a tiny woman, only five feet tall with brown eyes and light brown hair. She was generally featured in roles that cast her in an appealing sympathetic and nonthreatening manner. It was during the early years of movie making, 1939 on into the 1950's, that her fame was at its peak. Letters from fans arrived regularly. But usually they had been in praise of her work, never threatening.

Most of her roles cast her as the type of woman men immediately fell in love with. Not because of an innate sexuality like Marilyn Monroe, but because of her appealing and subtle femininity. Paul Gregory, her husband for the last twenty years of her life, described her as "tidy, like a delicate little butterfly." While this image contributed to her immense success in movies, it also had its downside. She discovered it was one thing to be admired from afar, the idol of the movie-viewing public and another to be pursued by obsessive individuals convinced through her screen performances that she was their personal sweetheart.

The second letter was postmarked Chicago. It was from the same man. Janet read only the beginning where he said he was coming to get her. She tore the letter into tiny pieces and threw them into the waste basket. She wasn't worried. The letters were simply from an overly ardent fan dreaming his fantasies.

Janet and Adrian's property seemed too remote for any stranger to find. Earl Stanley Gardner, the famous writer of the **Perry Mason** mysteries was Janet's godfather and owner of a ranch nearby. Lucien Hubbard owned a large spread less than a mile away and other celebrities were beginning to purchase land in this vicinity which while seemingly remote was only ten miles from the rapidly developing Hollywood atmosphere of Palm Springs.

Janet and Adrian's property had a small cabin. The only door to the outside opened directly into the kitchen. Beyond was a cozy seating and dining area, bedroom and bath. It was neither fancy nor spacious, just comfortable. Candles and lamps lit the dwelling at night since electricity was not yet available in this remote location. Water from the well was pumped into the house by a gasoline engine. When Janet and Adrian were away, a caretaker supervised the property, tended to the chicken house and monitored the pump so that trees on the property received the necessary irrigation.

Adrian and Janet coveted every moment they were able to spend at their cabin in the desert. Life there was so different from that of Hollywood film-making. Whenever Janet had a break from one of the many movies she was staring in, and Adrian was free from a costume designing assignment, they headed to the desert. But trouble was brewing.

The third letter came from Cheyenne, Wyoming, then one from Denver, Colorado and the next from Flagstaff, Arizona. It became clear an ardent suitor was making his way across the country with serious intentions. When a letter arrived from Blythe, California, no more than a day's drive away, Janet and Adrian realized the situation was serious and something had to be done. Not quite sure what to expect from the arrival of a stranger vowing to take Janet away with him, they turned to law enforcement for help. The Riverside County sheriff's department took the threatening letters seriously and advised Janet and Adrian to leave the cabin. A posse was formed to deal with the situation. The plan was to stake out the property and capture the suspect.

* * *

The sheriff's men found cover in clumps of bushes and trees as they settled in to wait and watch. It was not long after setting up the stakeout that a man was observed entering the gate. He walked boldly up the driveway and circled the building before entering the vacant cabin through the kitchen door.

On command, two of the posse members rushed from their hiding places firing warning shots ahead of them as they stormed into the building. Kicking open the bullet-ridden door, they stepped quickly inside, guns readied. On the floor in front of them with arms flung sideward lay the intruder, a pool of blood spreading outward on the linoleum floor. He had been killed by their gunfire after it passed through the wood and glass panel of the kitchen door.

* * *

While Janet's problem was solved, the abduction attempt and dead man in her house soured Janet on the remote cabin. She wanted nothing more to do with the desert property that had served as a happy hideaway. She and Adrian locked the door and never returned as a couple.

It wasn't until some years later after Adrian died and she met and married Paul Gregory that Janet began to think once again about the desert retreat in Seven Palms Valley near Desert Hot Springs. It seemed the right time to renovate the property and share it with Paul.

In the cabin, the old, blood-soaked linoleum was pulled up and replaced, but the door with bullet holes remained. Paul felt the scars on the door represented an historic event and they should be preserved. "We just painted over them," he said, "and ignored them."

However, Janet's problems were not over. Even into her seventies, she was stalked by another strange man convinced she should be his. While performing in the role of an elderly woman in **On Golden Pond,** a stage production playing in New York, she was accosted outside of her dressing room by a crazed man. He had entered through a back stage door and was actually frothing at the mouth, insisting he had waited fifty years to "capture his destiny" with Janet. This man was over eighty years old and he was still pursuing her! She directed stage security to bar him from her dressing room and they ultimately turned him over to the police.

It was Janet's manner, never hysterical or overwrought, that fueled her popularity. She was unprepossessing and affected people with her sincere warmth. These same qualities helped her at the beginning of her career to obtain bit parts in movies. While she supported herself working in a Los Angeles shoe store earning $18 a week, her small roles in comedy shorts gave her an entry into feature films.

Her big break came in 1926 when she was twenty years old and secured the lead role in the silent movie, *The Johnstown Flood.* From that success, she went on to win the first Academy Award for Best Actress. The year was 1928 and the award was for an incredible three major performances in one year. *Seventh Heaven* and *Street Angel* with costar, Charlie Farrell and *Sunrise* with George O'Brien. These were silent films. It was the first and only time an actress has won an award for three movies and until 1986, she was also the youngest.

As the tragic events at the cabin in Seven Palms Valley faded into distant memory, Janet was once again able to enjoy her desert retreat. Changes were made to the original building and grounds. In time the chicken house was remodeled into guest quarters, electricity installed when it became available in 1962. By then Janet's husband, Paul Gregory, was busy carrying out his plans for farming the land with beef cattle and raising squab for gourmet restaurants.

From a remote, dusty cabin, once the scene of a gruesome shooting, Singing Tree Ranch was born and blossomed into a successful working farm as well as an elite retreat for the rich and famous friends of Janet Gaynor and Paul Gregory.

MOBSTER HANGOUT OR MYTH
Al Capone

Al Capone, notorious gangster and bootleg liquor distributor of the 1920's prohibition era, lay asleep in his desert hideout. His movie star girlfriend, Gladys Walton, slept fitfully by his side. Capone's deep erratic snoring intruded on her brain as it filtered into her dreams of sun and sand and ocean waves lapping at her feet.

One series of especially loud snorts pulled her out of the dream, leaving her sleepy, but awake. As she lay stretched out on her back, deciding whether a gentle nudge would interrupt her lover's annoying nasal sounds, the soft creak of a floorboard registered in her consciousness. Immediately alert and without a moment's hesitation she used both hands to push Big Al off his side of the bed and with a swift turn away from him, she rolled like a log in the opposite direction. The momentum from her fall to the floor threw her body against the intruder's legs, throwing him off balance.

Her scream was lost in the noise of the gunshot and piercing crack of breaking glass, as the bullet meant for Capone slammed into a mirror attached to the dresser next to the bed. Within seconds, One Arm, Capone's personal bodyguard, burst into the room and with a single shot from his Colt revolver downed the would-be assassin. Big Al picked himself up off the floor, cursing and yelling about rival gangsters invading his place.

Gladys lay in a fetal position on the braided rag rug. Clinging to the sheet she'd pulled with her as she fell, she sobbed in breathy gulps. In the dark she felt the wetness, but couldn't see the blood seeping into her sheet where it touched the dead man sprawled *next to her. Big Al picked her up and laid her gently on the bed as he tenderly smoothed her hair away from her damp cheeks.*

"Hey, Baby, don't cry, you saved my life," he said, his voice hoarse with emotion.

* * *

Whether this story of an event at Two Bunch Palms Spa and Resort is true or a fabrication depends entirely upon which set of "facts" one chooses to believe. The story of the attack on Capone and Gladys lives on supported with tangible evidence in the Capone Cottage at the resort. The dresser with a bullet hole in its mirror was never replaced and guests in the Capone Cottage still see themselves in a reflection marred with spider web cracks emanating from a bullet hole. Some visitors request the Capone suite and a few insist it's haunted with his ghost. Others refuse to stay there and opt for one of the newer guest houses.

As the story goes, when Capone erected his hideout in the desert, there were no other houses or buildings within sight. Nothing but desert could be seen for miles, except two clusters of palm trees and a view of the surrounding mountains rising above the desert floor. It was the perfect place for Big Al's secluded fortress.

Capone is said to have built his stone house above a series of excavated tunnels large enough to conceal several cars. A turret or watch tower on the roof was manned by one of his mob. With no paved roads, a car driving on the gravel track to the property would kick up a cloud of dust easily observed when still far off in the distance.

Should the Feds decide to stage a raid, they would be seen from the stone house's turret while still miles away. By the time they pulled into the property, the black mobster cars would be safely stashed in the tunnels under the house. With all doors and windows shuttered and locked, the building would appear vacant.

It was a perfect hideout for Capone and he supposedly made multiple uses of it. As well as his personal love nest, good Canadian booze smuggled in via the Los Angeles Harbor was said to be stored there while waiting for distribution.

The 1920's were stormy years in the big cities with mob killings and vendettas against rival bootleggers. FBI agents trying to uphold liquor abstinence laws were caught in the middle. Gangster murders were commonplace in Chicago, Al Capone's home territory. In Los Angeles, Capone had powerful friends in the movie business, which is how he happened to be hanging around the set at Universal Studios that day in 1922 when Gladys Walton was filming. Capone became enamored with Gladys after seeing her in the silent movie, *The Untameable*. She was nineteen, already a star, he was twenty-three. Flattered by Capone's attention, Gladys went on a date with him and their relationship flourished in secret. Unfortunately for Gladys, when the news of her connection with Capone became known, Universal Studios canceled her contract. It was the end of her movie career. By then she had already starred in thirty-nine films.

The Capone story, myth or legend, was strengthened by the appearance in 2006 of John Walton from Yucca Valley, who claimed to be Capone's son. His mother was Gladys Walton. She passed away in 1993 at age 90. John says that although she told him the truth of his parentage when he was sixteen, she kept her secret from the world and wanted it revealed only after her death. With no longer a need to protect his mother, John embarked on a lecture tour and spent time at Two Bunch Palms attempting to prove his father's early presence there.

Capone never publicly admitted responsibility for fathering John, but he did visit Gladys in a Chicago hospital where John was born. According to Walton, when he was six years old, Capone arranged a marriage of convenience for Gladys with Henry Herbel as a measure of respectability. Gladys bore five more children during that marriage.

Finding a good balance between the truth and fiction of Two Bunch Palms' past is tricky, but some things are certain. The main dining room of the spa functioned at one time as a gambling casino. Its Neoclassic touches, remnants of Victorian furniture and Art Deco lighting fit the casino image. The small rooms on the lower level underneath the dining room are currently used for spa treatments, but functioned as a brothel in times past. And there are some old timers in Desert Hot Springs who still recall *"the day a group of pallid, hard-faced men in dark winter suits and snap brim fedora hats got off the train at Garnet Station and started driving across the desert."* (quoted from the spa's brochure) Local gossips didn't have to guess where these strangers were headed.

Kathryn Jordan collaborated with John Walton in writing Walton's story in a book entitled **Gladys and Capone.** Kathryn says she was shown a picture reported to have been taken in the late twenties. It shows a small stone house with two black cars parked next to it. Kathryn feels it is evidence of Capone's occupancy at Two Bunch Palms.

The myth of "Scarface" Al Capone and Two Bunch Palms is a compelling story easy to attach to this spa oasis in the desert. If Capone did build the first house on the property, he would be one of the earlier celebrities to find peace and quiet in the triangle of alluvial plain lying just northeast of Palm Springs.

For those who say the story is pure myth, evidence exists to prove their belief. In the archives of the Desert Hot Springs Historical Society an eight by ten black and white photo rests in a manila folder labeled "Two Bunch Palms." The photo is a shot of several clusters of palms taken from the northeast with Mt. San Jacinto in the far background. There are no buildings in the panoramic view, only the palm trees standing tall above rolling sand dunes dotted with creosote bushes. Penciled on the back of the picture is the date, 1937. If this date is correct and not a notation added at a later time, it would support the claims of those who insist Al Capone never used Two Bunch Palms as a hideout.

The biggest argument refuting the Capone legend are those old timers who swear there were no buildings at Two Bunch Palms until after the 1930's at which time Capone was already in prison for tax evasion. In an interview just two months before his death in 2009 at age 99, Frank Bogert, twice mayor of Palm Springs and a friend to movie stars and dignitaries, scoffed at the idea of Al Capone at Two Bunch Palms. "The Lipps owned that property," he said, "and there was nothing there in the 1920's. We used to ride our horses up there and picnic in the shade of the palms. All this talk about Capone is nonsense."

If that is true, then the question of who built the stone house with lookout turret and underground tunnels is still a mystery. John Walton claims to have proof of the subterranean car tunnels through a kind of computer imaging. A wooden door leading to a dirt tunnel, just large enough to accommodate a person still exists in one of the Capone House bedrooms. It stays locked. But what was its original purpose? Who put the bullet hole in the mirror and why hasn't an alternative story of Two Bunch Palms' early history come forth?

Even if continued research proves conclusively that Big Al was never at Two Bunch Palms, it may not be able to overcome the appeal of the colorful myth. Perhaps this picturesque desert retreat is so well-suited to its legendary mobster origin that no other explanation can compete with the lasting draw of the Al Capone legend.

Additional information to add another piece to the Al Capone puzzle came from Delinda Angelo, the owner of Glossy's, a resort wear boutique in Desert Hot Springs, who contributed this version.

* * *

"The other day at a Rotary Meeting, I was speaking to Jeff Bowman and for some reason the conversation drifted to Two

Bunch Palms. I have never attempted to correct the record on this matter because I didn't want to hurt anyone's feelings. However, I have thought about it and I realize that history belongs to everyone and I have an obligation to contribute when I have been a witness. My family has owned property in Sky Valley (East and adjacent to Desert Hot Springs) since February of 1962, when I started spending all of my vacations and weekends in Desert Hot Springs. I moved here full time in 1979."

"My father, Frank Gloss, along with Sam Weinberg, who built Sam's Family Spa on Dillon Road, and their gang of friends would take jeeps out in the desert. However, out on Bennett Road at the very top of the hill where 20th Avenue would cross if it went through, were 80 acres you could not go near. If you approached this property from any direction, two men in a jeep loaded with rifles would accost you and demand that you turn back. If you looked at the large house through binoculars you could see more men similarly armed. This property was called Bennett Ranch. Of course, this was very exciting to speculate about in the sleepy laid back desert. People would say, "It's a gangster hideout." Others would say, "Al Capone used to live there and now other mob guys have taken it over."

"None of this was the truth. What was true was that Harry Bennett, a top executive of Ford Motors had built his home there, and there was a great deal of labor unrest and violence. His sweet little wife, Josie, who died just a few years ago, stayed in that house for over 40 years. The armed men were just there for their protection until the labor problems were resolved.

"So along comes Chuck Beaumont, a man who was a genius at promotion. He purchased Two Bunch Palms Resort and suddenly, the hilltop rumor migrates six miles west. Voila, Al Capone and the gang is back. Mr. Beaumont and his lovely group would float into Johnny Costa's Desert Hot Springs Restaurant on Eighth Street in the biggest stretch limo you've ever seen, and proceed to spend enough money in our local economy that no one *would ever dare say anything different. Al Capone was at Two Bunch Palms and that was that!"*

Trading a Cad or a Jag for a Nag
B-Bar-H Ranch

Ask any local resident of Desert Hot Springs about celebrity hideaways and most likely the first name to come up will be the B-Bar-H Ranch located on Bubbling Wells Road just south of Dillon.

"You know, where the big stone entry gate is," they'll say and the next thing most commonly added is, "Mary Pickford had a home at the ranch, along with a lot of other stars. They used to have western dances and barbeques on Saturday nights. All of the big movie stars vacationed there."

The locals are right. The B-Bar-H was without doubt one of the favorite western style Hollywood hangouts in the desert from the 1930's through the 1950's. The registry at the ranch contained the autographs of an astounding array of people who were attracted to the B-Bar-H at a time when the dude ranch concept was new and exciting.

It all began in 1927 when Lucien Hubbard heard about the medicinal hot water found on desert land just north of Palm Springs. Hubbard, already a film company mogul, professional writer, and regular contributor to **Reader's Digest**, bought acreage from the Southern Pacific Land Company and proceeded to spread the word about his marvelous "find" in the desert. Following Hubbard's lead, other investors, including the famous mystery writer, Earl Stanley Gardner bought acreage nearby.

Charlie Bender, Hubbard's son-in-law, saw the land as an opportunity and partnered with him in the original purchase of

240 acres. Together they developed the B-Bar-H Ranch, "B" for Bender and "H" for Hubbard. In the beginning they grew citrus and dates and marketed them under the B-Bar-H brand.

Although Hubbard was a professional writer, he was also an outdoors man, which no doubt aided him in the years he spent as a war correspondent during World War 1. On his ranch in the California desert, his abilities as an expert rider and horseman were valuable assets for supervising his acreage. As he worked on developing buildings on his land, he constructed everything with a rustic western style. Stone buildings with red tile roofs, wood fences, a swimming pool, horse barn and corral beckoned early guests, who, by invitation only, began visiting the ranch. In the intimate circles of Hubbard's friends, the ranch became an elite getaway and so popular that in the late 1930's it was opened to the public.

On a Saturday night guests might mingle with stars like Bing Crosby, Bob Hope, Frank Sinatra, Joan Crawford and Rita Hayworth. During the week a trail ride or picnic could include Lew Ayres, Joan Fontaine, Monty Montana, Tyrone Power or Robert Taylor. Enjoying a meal in the dining room, one might see Olivia De Havilland, Peter Lorre, John Barrymore or Ronald Coleman. While at another time, Marlene Dietrich, Ray Milland, Preston Foster or one of the Marx Brothers could be seated nearby.

But it wasn't all movie stars who sought out the rustic tranquility of the ranch. Celebrities from the world of business, politics and international affairs included Bernard Baruch, Walt Disney, Darryl Zanuck and Jack Krinder, who owned the famous 21 Club in New York City.

Charlie Bender, Hubbard's partner, was the host and manager of the B-Bar-H. His wife organized activities including picnics, sports and daily riding parties that set out nearly every morning to explore what seemed to eastern guests as exotic desert terrain.

Saddled up on a well-trained horse that followed faithfully behind a leader was a perfect way to enjoy desert scenery.

However, there were some guests who preferred walking. When Mary Pickford stayed at the ranch, her custom was to go for walks by herself, but she frequently got lost. In her colorful flowing caftans, Mary must have looked like a human butterfly fluttering slowly across the dunes. At any rate, when Mary did not return after an hour or two, a search party would be organized to find her and escort her back to the ranch. It is not surprising that Pickford was treated so royally. She had starred in fifty-two feature films during the silent picture era and played bit parts in hundreds more. Born in Canada in 1892, she became "America's Sweetheart" and after her marriage to Douglas Fairbanks, the couple became unofficial ambassadors to the world because of their popularity.

Pickford flourished entirely in silent films. In 1929, she earned the second Academy Award given to a woman for *Coquette.* She retired from acting in 1933. However, as an astute business woman, she had already formed United Artists and continued to produce pictures. Pickford was forever a star and her presence at the B-Bar-H Ranch was never taken for granted.

In 1940 Jay Kasler, owner of the Free Sewing Machine Company, second only to the Singer Company, purchased the entire 240 acre ranch from Hubbard and Bender for $42,000. During World War II his company became the largest producer of ammunition in the U.S. After the war, he sold his company to the Japanese and founded City National Bank.

Kasler's family spent most of their weekends at the B-Bar-H and that is how his grandson, Richard Roger, grew up as an expert horseman, wise in desert lore. Roger's childhood was spent in casual contact with celebrities. He said he never thought of them as special and really didn't pay much attention to them. In his adult life, as a cardiologist and head of cardiology at Eisenhower

Hospital in Rancho Mirage for twenty-five years, many of the stars became his patients.

An advertisement in a 1940 magazine stated:

" You can't hardly find them no more," truly applies to a resort such as B-Bar-H Guest Ranch, a fast 10 miles removed from the hustle and bustle of downtown Palm Springs.

If you're looking for a "night club tan," then B-Bar-H is not the spread for you. If you see the wide, unfettered spaces, graced with the comforts, conveniences and services of a fine hotel without the tinsel, this is it. At B-Bar-H you'll trade a Cad or a Jag for a nag, swap high-glaring neon for low-hanging stars, swim in natural warm mineral water, enjoy the finest cuisine, sample the ultimate in the mixologist's art if you wish and sleep luxuriously in spacious cottages set in an oasis of tamarisk and palms."

With a mixture of prominent people in all walks of life, dress in the dining room was eclectic and fascinating. It was often possible to see swank evening clothes alongside outfits copied from real cowhands. But in general, people enjoyed dressing in informal western attire with boots, hat, skirt or jeans and shirt.

Inez Learnard, interviewed at age 103, said she remembers working at the the ranch one time when they were short of waitresses. She said, "Helen Haidet told me they needed some temporary help and she wanted me to go with her. So we filled in for several weeks in the dining room. The thing I remember most was how much in love Phil Harris and Alice Faye were. It was just so obvious looking at them. They even ordered the same thing at meals. I couldn't get over it. I also got to meet William Powell. Of course, I was used to seeing Janet Gaynor in the beauty shop. She was charming, always friendly, said hello, never ignored others. Can't say much for Charlie Farrell though. He was arrogant and never paid the bill, always left it for someone else." (Janet Gaynor and Charlie Farrell were paired together in so many movies, the public thought they should be married, but their relationship was purely on the screen.) Inez continued, "Oh, and I met Jack Dempsey who was there with his priest and manager. The thing I remember most about him was seeing him seated in an outdoor toilet with the door open."

An early ad from a 1939 edition of **Desert Magazine** described the ranch's location as "in the Coachella Valley near Palm Springs," with a mailing address of Garnet, named for Garnet Hill where small gemstones could be found lying right on the surface of the ground. At the time, there were no other established towns to the north, so Garnet became a catchall name for the big expanse of land surrounding Lucien Hubbard's holdings. For many years it was at Garnet where Southern Pacific trains rumbling through the desert, came to a stop as they dropped off passengers, mail and supplies.

Hired by the B-Bar-H when still a teenager, Joe Gottchalk, a local boy, met guests at the train station in Garnet. He loaded their monogrammed leather luggage into the ranch's wooden-sided station wagon and whisked them off to the B-Bar-H. He also served as desk clerk and bellhop, as well as delivering money to the bank and picking up groceries and mail. If there was a job to be done, Joe was ready. So the day a telegram arrived for Janet Gaynor at Singing Tree Ranch to the east, Joe rode his horse over the desert sands to deliver it.

Joe's duties included acting as chauffeur for B-Bar-H visitors who wanted to try their luck at the Dunes Club, a private membership gambling establishment in Cathedral City. The B-Bar-H ran its own card games and slot machines, but serious gamblers in those days went to the Dunes Club located on what is now Date Palm Drive and Highway 111. While only a distance of about ten to twelve miles on today's roads, in the 1940's it would have been a tedious ride over rutted, gravel tracks. But no one cared, they were out for a good time.

Organized trail rides took other visitors to favorite spots

like Seven Palms, Willow Hole and the oasis of Two Bunch Palms. Following a meandering dry streambed up a desert wash, stopping in the shade of a cluster of tamarisk trees for a picnic lunch packed in by wranglers, was a memorable experience for people from metropolitan New York, Philadelphia, Chicago or Los Angeles. Evenings at the ranch usually included a campfire after dinner, a favorite activity of many city dwellers.

Sometimes a visit to Cabot Yerxa's trading post provided enough entertainment for the day. Along with items he sold, Cabot amused his visitors with tales of his pet rattlesnakes and lizards. City people were entranced with a peek into the world of a true desert dweller and a way of life completely alien to them.

Sol Lessor, producer of the Tarzan films, found Cabot especially interesting. Lessor saw life in the desert related to his jungle movies. While the landscape was different, he saw similarities in Cabot's simple approach to daily activities.

If guests were not inclined to spend their time on horseback, there was an outdoor swimming pool and tennis courts. The ranch advertisements boasted:

"At B-Bar-H Guest Ranch you have civilized isolation. Ride, swim, sun laze and obey that recreational impulse with completely relaxed informality at the ranch. In a few minutes you can be at Chi Chi or the Doll House." (Two of the popular nite clubs in Palm Springs)

Rates which included meals were $8 to $15 per day on Monday through Thursday, but went up to $10 to $30 a day on weekends. For the very wealthy, deluxe bungalows with stone fireplaces could go as high as $30 to $75 a day, which for the time was quite pricey.

However, it was not necessary to stay at the ranch in order to mix with the stars. Saturday night barbeques were a highlight for anyone who wanted a night out with an assured good time. What could be more appealing than good, honest, homegrown food cooked outside under a desert sky, cowboy music spilling out from the western-themed ballroom, a starry night unimpeded by city lights.

Warner Baxter, owner of the Circle B Ranch on 20th Street, barely a stone's throw from the B-Bar-H, often came for the evening's events and brought along guests staying at his ranch. Baxter fit right into the western decor since he was well known for his role as the Cisco Kid, for which he won an Oscar in 1928.

Relaxation became the watchword at the B-Bar-H and somewhere along the way, the Code of the Pamperer sprang up. "Never to do today what can be done tomorrow." Louis Sobol was one of those who wrote about being initiated into the Order of the Pamperers. He starred in the film, *Copacabana* (1947) in which he played himself, Louie Sobol, a newspaper writer. Groucho Marx and Carmen Miranda were also in this black and white movie.

Poolside dining as well as lounging in the bright sun were exceptionally popular. No one wore a hat or sun shade. It was an innocent time with no worries about skin cancer or over exposure to the sun. The old idea that only field workers got tan, but women of society had lily-white skin was long gone. Tanning became an end in itself. Women appeared bronzed and golden while men lounged shirtless and hatless to become as brown as possible. Cigarettes were popular and smoking during dinner or while relaxing was the norm.

During the day, the stables were a popular place visited by the adventurous who wanted more than golf, tennis, badminton, shuffleboard or spending the afternoon around the pool. Every horse had a name and personality. Blaze, Cheyenne and Arky were favorites. The ability to ride one of the more spirited mounts was a way for many a male guest to prove himself, especially to those observing from behind the split rail fence.

Peter Lorre, an Austrian-American actor took naturally to

the horses. Unlike the sinister characters he portrayed, Lorre was gentle and kind with his mounts and popular at the ranch.

If horseback riding didn't capture a guest's desire, there was always the option of a jeep ride across the dunes. Jeeps were a novelty made popular by the war. Guests were easily amused by driving one around the horse corral just to get a feel for the vehicle. Often a friend was stationed at the fence to film the fun with one of the new amateur movie cameras.

By the 1950's Jay Kasler closed the ranch to the public and used it only for family and friends. The dude ranch concept had expanded throughout the West and was no longer unique to the B-Bar-H.

In 1976 Leonore "Lee" High bought the property. She had fond memories from earlier years of being invited to the ranch by Mary Pickford and actress, Ginny Sims. Her plans were to convert it to a school, but this never took place.

Instead, the historical B-Bar-H hideaway and playground of the elite and famous, languished until Modern Living Spaces, LLC purchased a part of it and built a cluster of Mid-Century Modern style homes. Few remnants of the original western ranch remain. The swimming pool has been filled in, the former recreational hall is occupied by a VFW Club and the beautiful old lodge with impressive stone fireplace and beamed ceiling stands forlorn and little used.

The most wistful reminder of the ranch and its illustrious clientèle is the original entrance sign – two stone pillars connected at the top with a rustic log from which hangs a wooden sign, B-BAR-H RANCH.

While ranch ownership has gone from one owner's paradise for elite guests, to many individual homes on separate lots, pride in the land and history remains. The Mid-Century Modern style of the new homes holds little in common with the original western decor. But current residents are proud of the ranch's history and strive to keep the ranch sign and stone pillars in good repair. They are quick to refer interested parties to their web site or the Desert Hot Springs Historical Society for information, where stories and memories of its glory days are preserved in historical archives. The famous visitors to the ranch are long gone, but nostalgia and reverence for times past cling to the B-Bar-H name and assure that it is not forgotten.

Celebrities not profiled elsewhere, but known to have visited the B-BAR-H

Lew Ayres	Sol Lessor
John Barrymore	Adolphe Menjou
Lionel Barrymore	Monty Montana
Wendy Barrie	Ray Milland
Frank Bogert	Sal Mineo
Joan Crawford	Eleanor Powell
Ronald Coleman	Tyrone Power
Jerry Colonna	John Raskob
Gary Cooper	Ginny Sims
Irene Dunne	Si Seadler
Preston Foster	Max Schuster
Rita Hayworth	Joseph Selznick
Beatrice Kaufman	Norma Shearer
Bonita Hume	Dore Schary
Sidney Kingsley	Robert Taylor
Mervyn Le Roy	Darryl Zanuck

WHITE OWLS AND MOVIE STARS
Two Bunch Palms Spa Resort

Generally resorts reek of publicity and extravagant testimonials prominently placed to lure the world to their doors. Two Bunch Palms Resort and Spa in Desert Hot Springs is different. History and mystery shroud its image like fogged glass framing an old photograph. The only information available to the public about this spa is descriptions of its nearly fifty specialized spa treatments and a tongue in cheek story about Al Capone using the place as his hideout during the early 1930's. The Egyptian clay body wrap using frankincense and myrrh and the Babassu sugar scrub spa treatments may have more substance than the Capone story, but both are irresistibly exotic. It really isn't necessary to get too inventive with various spa treatments at this resort, since Two Bunch Palms is blessed with natural hot mineral water of a quality considered rare and quite possibly the best in the world.

History of the exquisite water goes back to 1936 when a Dr. Augustus Broue having heard about the extraordinary hot water, came to Desert Hot Springs with one purpose, to study the naturally heated mineral water. After three years of scientific analysis, he declared it to be of superior quality, lithium-infused, unique and rare in the world. It is this water along with a strict privacy policy that draws the wealthy and well-known to Two Bunch Palms.

If it were possible to view the ferociously guarded clientèle list of the resort, it would include nearly every major movie star, musician and award winner in the entertainment industry as well as business moguls and celebrities from around the world.

A resident living near the resort once asked the manager, "Who's the big star at Two Bunch this week? I saw a stretch limo going through town yesterday, so I knew someone really big must be one of your guests."

The manager replied, "Big stars don't come in limos, they arrive in 4 by 4's and nondescript cars. They don't want to stand out. It's the "nobodies" and "wannabes" who come in flashy limos."

The resort has rules to accommodate celebrities. Talking softly, turning off all cell phones, no staring or asking for autographs. So even though some celebrities may talk about their experience afterward, they feel at ease while they're there knowing their privacy is guaranteed. And that's exactly the point of Two Bunch Palms' success as a hideaway for the famous.

Of course, it is possible to carry privacy issues even further as the Rolling Stones did in the 1980's when they took over the entire resort for a week and no one in the desert had the slightest inkling they were there. Or when Alexis Denisof and Allyson Hannigan (*American Pie* and *Buffy the Vampire Slayer*) had their wedding at the resort in Oct. 2003. They booked all fifty rooms as well as the entire resort facilities. They said their desire to be married at Two Bunch Palms was because it was the first place they had traveled to as a couple. While they kept their marriage ceremony very private, they described it later in public and allowed *People Magazine* to feature them on its cover.

Others like Ozzy Osborne, a heavy metal musician and songwriter, vacationed at the spa, but liked to go for walks around town. One day he wandered a few blocks down the street to Vons supermarket where he was recognized by other shoppers. As fans gathered around him, he autographed everything handed to him including grocery items. On his way back while passing the middle school, students were leaving for the day and he was besieged again. Ozzy put on his biggest smile and responded to the youngsters' requests until everyone who wanted an autograph was able to walk away with his personal signature.

A similar event occurred in 1985 when Tommy Lee and Niki Sixx of the Mötley Crüe settled down in the patio of McDonald's located in the same Vons supermarket shopping mall. They signed autographs and conversed with the gathered crowd, asking kids questions like, "What song do you like best?" and discussing their music with the eager group clustered around them. These public appearances are unusual for Two Bunch Palms' patrons. Most guests come specifically to enjoy the privacy of the elite resort.

The director, Robert Altman, was a frequent guest at the spa, which may account for his decision to film parts of *The Player* (a film released in 1991) at the resort. Tim Robbins' performance in the mud bath and some of the other romantic scenes are distinctly recognizable as Two Bunch Palms. The other movies Altman filmed in the Desert Hot Springs vicinity are at locations not so easy to recognize, partly because they are less well known and in some cases they simply no longer exist.

Questions continue. Which room did Douglas Fairbanks Jr. stay in? Who accompanied Charlie Chaplin on his visits? In more recent times, there was Anna Nicole Smith, who died in the Bahamas from a drug overdose. John Phillips with his daughter Mackenzie Phillips of *One Day at a Time* spent time there. Mackenzie has revealed her father abused her until their relationship became consensual. Whoops, there's a story that could rival the Capone myth, and this one could be substantiated. Barbara Streisand and her husband were seen having dinner in the restaurant by a local couple having a night out.

René Rousseau, who starred with Kevin Costner in the film, *Tin Cup,* stayed at the resort many times. These tiny glimpses pique the curiosity of celebrity watchers who want more, but are unlikely to get it.

The history of this watering hole in the desert goes back to its use by Native Americans. An 1855 section map shows an old Indian trail connecting Two Bunch Palms to Thousand Palms Oasis to the east where water also bubbles up to the surface. Both of these year around water sources sustain the growth of clusters of California's native fan palms, *Washingtonia filifera*. For early travelers, their shaggy green heads rose above the hot desert sands like natural billboards announcing the next water source and rest stop.

At the end of the 19th century the first land surveys were being conducted in the West, and by 1907 when the U.S. Army Camel Corps drew their official maps, they referred to the area as "where there were two bunches of palms." The name stuck and was shortened to Two Bunch Palms. The original section was further divided into smaller tracts as homesteading played out and land became desirable even if it was in the desert. Today, the resort occupies 56 acres of the entire 250 acre property.

The history of the property's ownership is vague. There is documentation showing that Southern Pacific Holdings sold the property in 1926 to an unnamed private entity who held it into the 1940's. This includes the disputed time when Al Capone is reported to have built his fortress at Two Bunch Palms, but records and authentication of his ownership are nonexistent and verification is impossible.

Frank Bogert, former cowboy mayor of Palm Springs, who passed away at age 99 in 2008, swore the Lipps family owned the property during the time Capone was supposedly there. He remembered many a horseback ride beginning at Smoke Tree Stables in Palm Springs that ended up at Two Bunch Palms for an afternoon picnic.

"There were no buildings there." He said. He scoffed at the idea of Al Capone ever being at Two Bunch Palms.

However, sometime in the 1940's construction did begin

to take place at the watering hole. The current dining room was built and operated as a casino with roulette wheel and private card games in a back room. A 1948 photograph of the building hangs at the Sidewinder restaurant in Desert Hot Springs. Few other specifics are known about this era although rumors claim the lower level spa treatment rooms were once a brothel.

One of the mysteries that tantalizes the imagination is the existence of underground tunnels that can be accessed from rooms 13 and 13A in the stone house which is attributed to Al Capone. The tunnels are large enough for a man to walk through and they have side branches off the the main run. A resort employee who grew up in the area, claims the tunnels continue in a southerly direction and at one time, emptied out on the lower edge of the dunes flanking the old Indian trail. It was thought the tunnels were an escape route that exited far enough away from the resort that a car could be waiting at the tunnel exit. The question arises, who was in need of such an elaborate escape system? With so little recorded information, history and mystery merge into an image clouded with tales of intrigue that tend to multiply as time goes by.

The sparsely recorded history of the resort confirms that at sometime in the late 1960's Two Bunch Palms was owned by a husband and wife team who ran the resort together. She cooked, he did the massages. They sold to Bob Beaumont, whose life was liberally interpreted in the movie, *Shampoo.* By the 1970's Two Bunch Palms was established as a resort for the elite who craved privacy and it has remained so ever since.

What actually goes on behind the gated entrance is and always will be a mystery that historical records will only get a peek at as the curtain drawn around the resort billows open now and then. The management remains true to its word and does not divulge who is there on any given date. They will admit only to having the guests who have already gone public on their own.

With all of its historical intrigue, there is one continuity at Two Bunch Palms which has been observed since its earliest days. One of the clusters of palm trees has been the home of families of white owls for as long as anyone can remember. For some mysterious reason, they are attracted to this location. Certainly the water is important, but even with many other water sources available today, white owls still nest in the same palms as they did 100 years ago. Celebrities may come and go, but the owls are a constant.

Two Bunch Palms Spa has been featured in *Spa Magazine, Conde Nast Traveler* and every major travel publication at least once every year. The resort may not have been Al Capone's hideout, but it most certainly has been a hideaway for a multitude of celebrities some with notorious reputations.

The air of intrigue over Two Bunch Palms remains thick with promise. Perhaps someday its secrets will be revealed, historical gaps filled in, myths and rumors confirmed or discounted, new liaisons reported. But for now, fanciful speculation merely enhances the glamorous image of this desert hideaway across the wash from Palm Springs.

Frightening Roles Pay Off
Peter Lorre

Peter Lorre was one of the regulars at the B-Bar-H Ranch during its heyday. Lorre was a good horseback rider and could be counted on for good company. Lorre's life as a guest at the B-Bar-H Ranch must have stimulated a multitude of jokes based on the nefarious characters he played. He was never known to complain and no doubt joined in the fun. At the funeral of Bela Lugosi in 1956, Lorre and Vincent Price joined other Hollywood mourners, and Lorre, with his typical sense of wry humor, suggested to Price, "Do you think we should drive a stake through his heart just in case?"

Born in 1904 into a Jewish family in Hungary, he was named Laszlo Lowenstein. His acting career began in Vienna when he was seventeen. At a slight 5 ft. 5 in. and speaking exclusively German, his first major role and the one which defined many of his future movie personas, was the 1931 film *M* in which Fritz Lang cast him as a child killer.

When the Nazis took over Germany in 1933, Lorre moved to Paris and then London where he caught the attention of Alfred Hitchcock's associate producer. In spite of his speaking mostly German, he was cast in *The Man Who Knew Too Much* (1934) and learned his lines by phonetically pronouncing the English words.

It was, no doubt, his foreign accent which endeared him to audiences when he ended up in Hollywood playing foreigners with suspect intentions. He was cast as a Japanese detective in the *Charlie Chan* series and as *Mr. Moto* in another. While he didn't care for these roles, they did give him an American fan base which contributed to his selection for a major part in the *Son of Frankenstein* (1939). Ultimately, Lorre became ill and Basil Rathbone ended up replacing him in the movie.

His career unfolded as he continued to gain roles as a main character in suspense and mystery films. He co-starred with Bela Lugosi and Boris Karloff in *You'll Find Out* (1940), played Joel Cairo in *The Maltese Falcon* (1941) and Ugarte in *Casablanca* (1942) with Humphrey Bogart and Ingrid Bergman. He went on to star with Sidney Greenstreet in *Three Strangers* (1946) and as Dr. Einstein in *Arsenic and Old Lace* (1944).

After World War II, his popularity in Hollywood declined and he returned to radio and stage work in Germany. By 1954 he was back in the U.S. and became the first actor to play a James Bond villain in a television spoof of "**Casino Royale.**" Also, in 1954 he joined Kirk Douglas and James Mason in *20,000 Leagues Under the Sea.*

Lorre died in 1964 at age fifty-nine and even though he was married three times, he had only one offspring, a daughter, Catharine. It was after Lorre's death that Catharine endured a horrendous experience. She was stopped by two men disguised as police officers. Their intent was to kidnap and murder her. When they found out she was Peter Lorre's daughter, they abandoned their plan and let her go. It was not until Kenneth Bianchi was arrested as the Hillside Strangler in 1977 that Catharine learned her would-be abductors were Bianchi and his cousin. Bianchi confessed to the aborted abduction and murder plan. What he didn't make clear, was their reason for letting her go after discovering she was Peter Lorre's daughter. One possibility is they were afraid the publicity generated by the killing of a woman related to a well-known movie star would lead to increased efforts to find and arrest them. Or is it possible they were fans of Peter Lorre?

Considering the roles Lorre played in suspense and crime films and especially his first big success in *M* where he portrayed a serial killer who preyed on little girls, it seems ironic that his own daughter narrowly escaped a horrible death from a serial killer entirely on the basis of being his daughter. Surely Lorre could never have anticipated how real life imitates fiction, that after a career of playing roles in movies involving vampires, murderers and shady characters, his own influence would extend from his grave to save his only child.

MOBSTERS, CARD GAMES AND THE SOCIALLY ELITE
Ray Ryan

Ray Ryan, a man with a melodic name and personality to match played a major role in the desert celebrity scene during the late 1940's, 50's and 60's. As one of a seventeen-man group who purchased and remodeled the famous El Mirador Hotel and Spa in Palm Springs, he quickly rose to prominence in desert society. Through his establishment of the El Mirador as the social center of the newly evolving resort community and through his land purchases and contact with both movie and business celebrities, Ryan rapidly attained the status of "Mr. Palm Springs."

Although he never gave up his home in Evansville, Illinois, he still managed to spend enough time in the desert to support local charities and keep his name near the top of the desert celebrity list. He was involved with the development of the Bermuda Dunes Country Club, North Shore Yacht Club on the Salton Sea and numerous housing tracts throughout the Coachella Valley.

Unlike some other prominent people, Ryan didn't come to Desert Hot Springs to hide out. That was never his style. He had a business deal in mind – land that would yield money to help support his extravagant lifestyle. He saw great potential for the 2,500 acres he purchased just west and slightly north of Desert Hot Springs. Natural hot water, panoramic mountain views and slightly cooler temperatures than in Palm Springs made the property an especially attractive investment for a developer. Not that Ryan wasn't already wealthy from his oil leases in Indiana. It was said they earned over $10,000 a day, more than enough to finance his varied projects.

As an oil man, Ryan didn't suffer during the depression. Oil and gambling were big back in Evansville. A local banker reported Ryan would come in to pick up $10,000 just for "walking around" money. During the 1940's Evansville, in the heart of the Midwest, flourished with nightclubs, gambling and red light districts. It was said that more horse rooms and gambling dives per capita were located there than any other city in the nation.

Ryan was able to hobnob with the big money in any city he chose to visit including overseas. On a trip to Africa, in 1958, he was not satisfied with the accommodations at the Mt. Kenya Safari Club and ended up buying the hotel the next day. William Holden, the actor and Ryan's friend, suggested the purchase when Ryan complained relentlessly about the service. With Holden as his partner in the venture and Ryan's connections, the Safari Club charter members soon included the elite, the rich and famous. Notables like Winston Churchill, President Eisenhower, Henry Ford, Walt Disney, Clark Gable, John Wayne and Joan Crawford were listed, as well as at least eighteen people known to be in top positions in the New York mob.

Ray Ryan was a gambler, a big time gambler, and it ultimately became his downfall. According to Frank Bogert, the colorful cowboy who served as both mayor and social celebrity of Palm Springs, Ryan bet on every college football team and played cards with East Coast and Midwestern Mafia kingpins. Bogert said, "The Mafia were the only ones who could afford the high stake games Ryan liked. He had to have someone rich enough to make it interesting for him."

It may have been one of these poker games that sealed Ryan's fate. He played five card stud for five days with Nicolas, "Nick the Greek," Dandolos in Las Vegas, and walked away with winnings of $500,000. Ryan's card game with Dandolos became so famous that Ian Fleming used it as a basis for his James Bond book, *Goldfinger* (1959) which was also made into a movie starring Sean Connery. Unfortunately for Ryan, it also became the catalyst for his murder years later.

Dandolos was a sore loser and after his massive loss, accused Ryan of cheating. The Las Vegas mob sided with Dandolos. After that things were never the same. For the next twenty-eight years Ryan's life was plagued with schemes to extort money from him, and attempts to kidnap and do away with him.

One effort to kidnap Ryan and rough him up, maybe even do him in, took place in the Sands Hotel, Las Vegas and nearly succeeded. Two hired thugs loitered in the lobby of the Sands Hotel and waited for Ryan to appear. They intended to quietly saunter up to him, one on either side and walk him out of the building into their parked car outside. Just as they planned, Ryan stepped out of the elevator, alone and vulnerable. But as they approached side by side, Ryan sensed something was amiss. He quickly scanned the room and spotted a man and woman dressed in wedding attire, arm in arm, entering from the hallway. Using the newlyweds as a shield, Ryan darted behind them and raced down the corridor. The two would-be kidnappers hesitated for only a fraction of a second, but it was enough for Ryan to escape as the bride and groom, perplexed by the sudden burst of activity, tried to figure out what was going on.

Months later after the FBI got involved, the two thugs hired to make the hit were found and arrested. It was Ryan's testimony that sent them to prison for eight years. However, that wasn't the end of it. His troubles with the gang had merely begun. Eastern mobsters controlled by the Mafia were migrating west and multiplying in Las Vegas as casinos sprouted on the "strip" like wildflowers after a rain in the desert.

Gang syndication control begun by Al Capone in Chicago with his bootleg liquor distribution business begun in 1920 during the prohibition era, served as a model for other mobsters.

Chicago held the high score for gangland killings with 986 murders attributed to the mob between 1919 and 1964. But as turf wars escalated and gang killings became regular occurrences, Ryan, along with his gambling buddies, many of whom were mobsters, found himself part of that continuing scene. Las Vegas was heating up, not just with high summer temperatures, but with the number of people who disappeared attempting to stand up to the mob after winning too often or too much in the casinos.

Over the years Ray spent large blocks of time in Palm Springs supporting charitable causes and enjoying the desert social scene, in spite of his gambling interests which linked him with mobsters like, Marshall Caifano, "Jimmy the Weasel" Fratianno, Sam Giancana, Charles Delmonico, and Frank Costello as well as "Nick the Greek" Dandolos who had begun the vendetta against Ryan by accusing him of cheating.

Ryan's life was characterized by extravagance, excitement and danger. His extreme wealth and likable personality made him popular in social circles. However, his association with mob bosses and gambling buddies, put him in constant danger from extortion schemes to outright murder. His wife, Helen, once said, "Ray's never happy unless he is walking on the edge."

Some of the elaborate and convoluted plots involving Dandolos' attempts to get his money back from the card game where he thought Ryan had cheated, were even worked out in prison cells by Mafia members the FBI was able to put away, usually for tax evasion. But the syndicate's associations and motives were so varied and intricate, it was often impossible to figure out the connections.

Fortunately for Ryan, along with his mobster enemies, he also had mobster friends who shielded him from those who wanted him dead. But by 1977 Ryan's "buffers" had passed away, most of them killed gangland style and his enemies were able to carry out their plans to get revenge.

Back in his home city of Evansville, one day in 1977, Ryan parked his car outside of the spa where he swam and exercised. As usual, he handed his gold necklace with gold coins and a medallion to spa manager, David Newcomb, to put in a lock box for safe keeping while Ryan swam in the pool and worked out with weights. Newcomb's dad, Kenneth Newcomb happened to be at the spa that day and made arrangements with Ryan to look at some real estate.

After finishing his workout and retrieving his gold jewelry, Ryan left the spa with Kenneth Newcomb. But before they could go to view the properties, Newcomb remembered a brief errand he needed to take care of. He suggested Ryan wait in his car outside the spa. Newcomb drove off in his own vehicle and was only about four blocks away when he heard the blast. A bomb planted underneath the chassis of Ryan's Lincoln Continental Mark V had exploded and torn the vehicle into multiple pieces. The only way the remains of Ryan's body could be identified was by his signature piece of jewelry, the gold necklace.

The Evansville police department investigated the murder and called in the FBI, but after following lead after lead for ten years, neither group had substantial evidence to prove who did it. Not until over twenty years later in 1999 after years of digging by an Evansville police detective named Bagbey, did the details of Ryan's death surface. Even though information indicated clearly who triggered the bomb that killed Ryan, the government was still not able to prove conclusively who the killers were. Bagbey admitted the chances of anyone being charged for the murder were very remote since much of the information came from federal informants. Ryan's life of gambling and high stakes investments had infused his life with danger and it finally caught up with him. Ryan, himself, said, "They'll get me some time. I know it."

At the time of his death, Ryan's 2,500 acres in Desert Hot Springs were still raw desert, consisting mainly of acres of creosote bushes, cholla cactus and drifting sand. But if his heirs were to visit the property today they could play a round of golf on the manicured course meandering through a community of paved streets and neatly landscaped desert homes. The sign on the block wall surrounding the property reads Mission Lakes Country Club.

CELEBRITY MAGNET
Cabot Yerxa

The train pulled to a jerky halt at Seven Palms Station, also called Garnet. The young boy just ten years old, awoke as a heavy jolt accompanied by voices and metallic sounds replaced the repetitive sway of the locomotive. Eager to experience everything, the boy slid quietly from his reclining train seat and walked down the aisle to the end of the car. The heavy door to the corrugated metal platform opened with a noisy rattle and thunk as he pressed down on the latch and pushed hard. He stepped out into another world entirely different from anything he had seen before. It was after midnight, but a full moon cast its pale glow over a world of undulating mounds of desert sand in every direction, an alien landscape dotted with a few low bushes and spiky plants. Not a single building was within sight and in the far distance dark mountainous shapes loomed over the horizon. A lone coyote barely visible in the weak moonlight trotted off until it disappeared over a rounded dune. Unsaid words formed in the boy's head. This is a strange and scary place. I'm glad we're not getting off here. Little did he know that he would spend most of his adult life in this very desert less than ten miles to the north of Garnet Station.

It was 1893 and the young Cabot Yerxa and his family were on their way to spend three months in Mexico, where his father was involved with a new concept in housing development. On this trip, the Yerxas were honored by President Porfirio Diaz with the presentation of a framed picture depicting the national seal of Mexico, an eagle perched on a cactus with a snake in its beak It was made entirely of feathers including the flowing writing. Over a hundred years later this exquisite feather picture can still be viewed in Cabot's preserved pueblo home in Desert Hot Springs.

It would be impossible to tell stories of celebrities who came to the desert during the early days of the twentieth century without including the tale of Cabot Yerxa. Of all the wealthy, famous and talented people who chose the area for a permanent home, Cabot's is one of the most colorful and varied. The uninformed have called him a desert rat, but those who knew him were more likely to see him as an American Renaissance man. A true pioneer, friend of native Americans, architect, painter, theosophist, builder and recycler, he was sought after by nearly every other celebrity who visited the area.

Cabot's story begins with his birth in 1883 on the Lakota Sioux Indian Reservation. He was already distinctive as the first white child born in the Dakota Territory. The last buffalo hunt had taken place the year before in 1882 and North Dakota did not become a state until 1889. But by the time Cabot was born his father, Fred Yerxa, had already migrated west and was operating a trading post in Souix territory.

One of the Yerxas' Dakota Territory friends was William "Buffalo Bill" Cody who spent many a night as guest in the Yerxa home. He even carved a special high-seated chair for young Cabot. As the boy grew, Cody carved the seat lower to accommodate the child's height. This chair and another upholstered with buffalo hide and given to the Yerxas by Cody have survived as part of Cabot's household furniture and are on view at Cabot's Pueblo Museum.

During the Yerxas' stay in the Dakota Territory another adventurous man operated two ranches there, the Maltese Cross and the Elkhorn. His name was Theodore Roosevelt and years later he would play an important role in Cabot's life.

Cabot's mother, Nellie Cabot of the Boston Cabots, named her baby after her uncle, Henry Cabot Lodge. Cabot's father, Fred Yerxa (an Americanized version of the Dutch *Juerckse*), came from one of New Brunswick's first families. The new baby, with genes inherited from two historic and influential families, followed his ancestors in exploring new lands, developing his multitude of talents and cultivating famous friends. His achievements over the eighty-six years of his life would be a credit to anyone, but they also brought the respected Cabot name from Boston to the far west and the entrepreneurial skills of the Yerxas to the desert at a time when desert living was still in the pioneer stage.

Cabot's early childhood was spent as the only non-Indian child on the reservation and it was here he learned respect and understanding of Native Americans. North Dakota had been a state for less than a year and Cabot was a mere seven years old when the tragic killing of Sitting Bull in 1890 clawed a raw wound in the hearts of Native Americans.

It was only three years later when the ten-year old Cabot saw the desert for the first time when the train he and his family were taking to Mexico made its stop at Garnet Station and only five years after that when the San Francisco Chronicle's explosive headline, "Gold Discovered in Alaska!" took hold of young Cabot and wouldn't let go.

Since his father felt he was too young to follow the other gold seekers to Alaska, Cabot heeded his advice, stayed at his home in San Francisco, saved his money for a year, and at sixteen was on his way to the Klondike with a few warm clothes and a trunk full of cigars manufactured in Cuba by his family's brand, **Yerxa's Opera.** Merchandising came naturally to him from his family's experience with grocery stores in major cities including Fargo, Boston, and San Francisco. After only three summers at his small stand in Nome in the Alaskan gold country, he had made $30,000 selling cigars for six dollars each that cost him two cents apiece. By the age of nineteen, Cabot had made his first fortune.

Money, however, was not the only pursuit of teenaged Cabot. In order to learn about native Alaskans, he lived with an Inuit family and learned their language. Discovering there was no written version, he invented a 320 word vocabulary and sold it word by word to the Smithsonian Institution. This has been verified by the Smithsonian, but whether it was for five cents or fifty cents a word is still in question. Languages seemed to come easily to Cabot and during his lifetime he would speak five: Sioux, Inuit, Spanish, English and French.

It was in Alaska, at a Dawson City Masonic gathering that Cabot met Teddy Roosevelt, soon to become the twenty-sixth President of the United States. Cabot, only sixteen, was certainly not a Mason. But somehow, he managed to borrow a sash and hat and insert himself into the back row of their formal group picture with Teddy Roosevelt prominently seated front row center.

His extraordinary success in Alaska continued after he returned home from his Alaskan adventure. A request to the newly-elected President Theodore Roosevelt landed him a government job as Postmaster (1908 to 1911) in Sierra Madre. The President's ties with the wild west were demonstrated when Geronimo, famous Native American, rode in the President's inaugural parade. No one then could have guessed Geronimo would die four years later as a prisoner of war in 1909.

Cabot's marriage to his first wife, Mamie, took place in 1908. Along with the handsome young Cabot, Mamie loved the position of authority he held at the post office and their connection with the Roosevelts. A signed formal portrait of the Presidential family was proudly displayed at the Yerxa home and still hangs on the wall of Cabot's Pueblo in Desert Hot Springs.

But in the great California Sonoran Desert momentous events were also taking place. It was in 1905 when the Colorado

River broke through an irrigation canal and began forming the Salton Sea, a body of water soon to have a profound affect upon the surrounding desert and by 1911, Cabot, bored with his government job in Sierra Madre, heard about the flourishing citrus industry in Redlands. He, along with his father and brother decided to invest their entire fortunes in orange groves. They had no warning of the disaster waiting to strike. A major freeze came through the next year and not a single orange tree survived, wiping out the Yerxa's entire investment. The Yerxa family was ruined. Cabot's father died soon after, his brother moved to San Francisco and opened a grocery store. Cabot had nothing left other than his determination.

It made sense to Cabot when Bob Carr, a friend, told him about homesteading possibilities on western lands and convinced him to try it in the Coachella Valley. The year was 1913. He left Mamie behind and set out with Carr to start over. Once again he boarded the train and for the second time arrived at Garnet Station. On this day he and Carr walked away from the steaming giant and headed north into the desert. The pack on Cabot's back contained little more than a blanket and a few cans of beans. They were so unprepared they hadn't thought to include a can opener. It was only through the help of an already established lady homesteader who took them in and fed them that they were able to survive and ultimately establish separate claims.

Cabot didn't have the $10 fee needed to file for a homestead, but he had acquired some skill in painting and discovered that his postcard-sized scenes painted on wood appealed to tourists at Garnet Station. His new life began to take shape.

The 160 acres he chose to homestead was located just east of Two Bunch Palms oasis. His first nights on the property were spent sleeping on the ground, then in a hole in the hill. When he had saved enough from odd jobs, he purchased a burro for ten dollars and named her "Merry Christmas " because he felt she was a gift to him. He allowed her to wander loose in the desert and when he wanted her for work, he'd ring a bell and she would appear. She always returned at dinner time to share his own meals of potatoes and beans. She shared Cabot's life and even learned to drink beer from a bottle and chew tobacco.

Finally he managed to build a makeshift one room 10x12 foot cabin using castoff remnants of wood. At the time, there were only nine other families in the area. A year later, he constructed his "Eagle's Nest" cabin of stone. It was 10x20 feet. But he still had to walk seven miles each way with Merry Christmas three times a week to get water at Garnet. Why he didn't get water from Two Bunch Palms oasis is a mystery. Perhaps he thought it wasn't potable or didn't know that palm trees growing naturally in the desert signal a water source.

It was about this time he met and became friends with Carl Eytel, a Palm Springs artist whose work is coveted and collected today. Cabot and Eytel roamed the desert together painting the magnificent scenes spread out before them. Cabot once said of Eytel, "Carl was peace itself." Painting was an artistic endeavor Cabot would pursue throughout his life. Seldom able to buy ready made paints, he developed his own from desert minerals and plants. The formula for each color was carefully transcribed in a notebook he kept in his paint box. The same palette, colors and tones were used for all of his paintings. Many he gave away, others he sold. A few were stolen from his home after his death, but some still remain on the walls of his preserved historic pueblo.

It was while living in his "Eagle's Nest" that Cabot dug his first well. As the story goes, he dug deeper and deeper in the earth until the ground was so hot he had to stand with each foot in a separate bucket of cold water in order not to burn his feet. Concerned about the temperature increasing so greatly as he dug deeper, he had a rope tied around his waist with instructions to his friend Bob Carr to pull him out quickly should he give a yell. At about thirty-five feet, he hit water, but its temperature was above the boiling point and he decided it wasn't good enough to drink.

It was then an elderly Indian directed him to try digging about 600 feet away from the first well. This one yielded cold water. Thinking how miraculous that was, he named the place Miracle Hill, a name that remains today on the city street cresting the hill where Cabot dug his first wells.

However, the hot and cold water so close to each other is not a miracle, but a natural phenomenon due to an earthquake fault running through the area. Cold water seeping down underground from the Little San Bernardino Mountains is found on one side of the fault and water heated from the magma underlying the fault is trapped on the other. Both are crystal clear and pure with no smell of sulfur as is often found in hot springs.

Now that Cabot had a home and water, he brought Mamie and his son, Rodney born in 1914, to his desert home. Mamie was unimpressed. A dirt floor, windowless walls and lack of comforts did not suit her. After a short time, she took Rodney and went back to the city. They never did reconcile or live together again.

Cabot's life changed even more as World War I broke out and the US entered the fight in 1917. By October of 1918 Cabot had enlisted in the army. He turned Merry Christmas loose because he couldn't bear to sell her, his trusted companion, even though he was offered $100 for her. He closed the door on Eagle's Nest, and boarded the train at Garnet Station.

In the army, Cabot never saw combat. But he served under Lieutenant Dwight D. Eisenhower in the tank corp and became friends with the second person in his life to become president of the United States. The invitation for Cabot and his second wife, Portia, to attend Eisenhower's inaugural ball remains in the archives at Cabot's Pueblo.

After leaving the army, Cabot once again served as postmaster, but this time in Frutilla, a small town near Blythe on the California, Nevada border. His heart was not in it and he returned to Europe to attend the *Academie Julien* in Paris where

Matisse and other French impressionists studied. One of his series of desert scenes is reminiscent of Monet's haystack series, the same scene painted at different times of day with different light. His travels around Europe and to South America added more knowledge and experience to this man of many interests and friends.

During the ten year period between 1926 and 1936 when Cabot was back in the U.S. running a retail store in Moorpark, the horrendous stock market crash occurred that caused the great depression, Joshua Tree National Monument was established by Franklin Roosevelt and Cabot's artist friend, Carl Eytel died. Eytel was so respected by the Cahuilla Indians they allowed him to be buried in their tribal cemetery.

Moorpark in Ventura County, the location of Cabot's general store, was a long way from the desert where Cabot had homesteaded and built Eagle's Nest, but fate came calling once again and dangled a lure calling him back to that "strange place" he, as a ten year old boy, had first seen from the train at Garnet Station.

It was in Moorpark that Cabot met L.W. Coffee, a Los Angeles developer and told him about the hot water in the desert. Coffee was intrigued and decided to buy land to develop a health and wellness community around the curative hot water concept. By then, a grid for the town of Desert Hot Springs had been set up, but the population was still under 100.

Not until 1941 did Cabot arrive by train for the third time at Garnet Station. But this time he was back in the desert to spend the rest of his life constructing his Hopi-inspired pueblo home which stands today in homage to both the Native Americans Cabot revered so fervently and to Cabot himself although that was never his intention. His amazing story paralleling western expansion and pioneering in the desert dovetails with a wide variey of other celebrities who spent time in this undeveloped swath of dunes and creosote away from the urban centers of social activity.

Cabot was fifty-six when he settled on new property north of his original Eagle's Nest on Miracle Hill and began building his pueblo in homage to the Native Americans he knew and understood. Samu, the last Chumash medicine man, became a close friend and Cabot worked with him for rights of Native Americans. The first room he constructed took into account the sensitivities of his Indian friends. While the walls were built of adobe bricks he made from local clay with a handful of concrete thrown in, and the fireplace was stone, he left bare earth for the floor. When his Indian friends visited, they slept on that earthen floor because it was their belief that all good things come from mother earth. It was also helpful in hot weather to sprinkle the dirt floor with water and thereby bring about cooling through evaporation.

Everything Cabot did in the building of his home was thought out and planned to fit in the desert and use the desert climate. He spent the first year digging into the side of a hill for the ninety-foot long east side of the building. The concrete wall built into the hill was two feet thick and windowless. The earth of the hillside cooled the building and no morning sun could enter to heat the interior. Windows were planned to be opened for prevailing breezes and a duct built into the ceilings of the rooms vented hot air. Telephone poles, old railroad ties, deadwood, even driftwood collected from a flood at the All American Canal near the Salton Sea were scavenged from the desert and used in the building. Rusty, bent nails were pounded straight and reused. Glass in whatever shape he found it became part of a window; the frame and mullions were cut to fit. Of the 150 windows in the four-story unfinished building, none are alike. The same is true of the sixty-five doors and thirty-five rooms. But aside from the recycling of materials, Cabot built using the principle of asymmetry. He believed in the Native American idea that symmetry suppressed the human spirit and above all his work was meant to foster creativity, rather than suppress it.

It is never too late for true love and Cabot found his when he was sixty years old and met Portia Graham, a spiritual guidance counselor. She was a Rosicrucian and a Unitarian. She taught theosophy and personality enhancement. By then Cabot was himself a thirty-second degree Mason, Their interest and philosophies dove-tailed and Cabot pursued Portia with love letters and poetry for two years before she finally agreed to marry him and move into his hand-built home on three conditions: modern conveniences in kitchen and bath, and her own private living quarters. They were married in 1945, four years after Cabot began work on his pueblo and the year World War II ended. Desert Hot Springs had its first official post office, but there would not be street lights nor telephone lines for another four to five years. The city would not be incorporated until 1963.

It is fair to say that along with all of Cabot's friends and visitors, many of whom were celebrities, Portia brought famous people to the pueblo, as well. She had a devoted friendship with Rabia Martin, the first person to bring the Sufi movement to the United States. Another intimate friend was Ivy Duce who became leader of the Sufi movement thirty-five years later. Both Cabot and Portia traveled to Ojai to meet and attend a lecture by noted theosophist, Krishnamurti.

Their library contained books ranging from the Bhagavad-Gitas, Bibles, Kabalas, Vedic, Sufi and Christian writings. Both Cabot and Portia were scholars and in a love letter to Portia, Cabot wrote, "...[We] could perhaps create a new world to live for in the future different from any other pattern you know or others to follow." While Cabot built studio rooms for artists and writers to visit, Portia taught manners and etiquette in a third story space outfitted with built in benches and an altar.

Cabot and Portia were open and eager to experience ideas

that stretched the mind. Together they became interested in UFO's through the influence of George Van Tassel, who designed and built a high-voltage electrostatic generator in the high desert near the town of Landers. Van Tassel's intent was to recharge human cell structure like a fountain of youth and eventually he envisioned time travel. His thirty-eight-foot-high, fifty-five-foot diameter Integratron is located near seven-story Giant Rock, a massive curved boulder under which Van Tassel lived and held UFO conventions in the 1950's. According to Cabot's notes, a narrow winding stairway from Portia's second floor apartment leading up to a small cubicle on level three was used for viewing sunsets, trysts, and star-gazing.

When Cabot opened his pueblo style home as a museum in 1954, he kept a guest book which contains some very famous names. Tennessee Williams, playwright of *Cat on a Hot Tin Roof,* signed their guest book along with Irene Selznick and many others from the nearby B-Bar-H Ranch. Cary Grant would have left his signature in the guest book if Cabot hadn't kicked him out due to a misunderstanding. Louis Sobol wrote about Cabot in *The New York Journal American.* Roy and Marie Ropp were frequent guests. Roy created and directed the first Pageant of the Masters in Laguna Beach. Burt Proctor who became known for his paintings of cowboys, always included a sketch when he signed his name. Sometimes he also listed the items he'd brought as gifts, such as paints, magazines and food. Jan Wampler, architect and professor at MIT included Cabot in his book, *All Their Own,* which notes that, "In the hands of innovative designers, ordinary materials are transformed into extraordinary shelters." This sentence perfectly describes Cabot's pueblo and helps define the interest visitors took in the unique structure.

The collection of artifacts given to Cabot by his friends may tell the story of his associates as well as or better than names in the guest book. Fifteen hundred-year-old Anasazi pottery, beaded relics from the Little Big Horn area in Montana, Edward

Curtis photographs, ivory carvings from Alaska, paintings, Indian blankets, an autographed Mark Twain book are but a few of the preserved items.

An appraiser from Indianapolis was hired in 2008 to assess the collection. She expected to spend several days but found that after two weeks of continuous work, she still wasn't finished. She told The Desert Sun, " There's some real depth, it's not just coming to see a pretty collection. It really is significant.....It's pretty neat that this has been able to survive all this time." She also stated that the "Yerxa's is the most varied collection she's seen compiled by just two people – Yerxa and his wife, Portia."

The artifacts, personal effects, and building itself are rich in the history of the western desert during the early and middle years of the twentieth century. There is no doubt Cabot and Portia, with their varied interests and intellectual pursuits played key roles in attracting celebrities to the Desert Hot Springs area. But as time passes, changes take place.

In March of 1965, eighty-two year old Cabot sat in his usual chair at the small wooden table in the kitchen of the pueblo. The room originally constructed with a primitive stove and a sink outfitted for recycling gray water to the outside garden, now contained a real Norge refrigerator and updated cooking facilities. These were Portia's requests when she agreed to the marriage. She recognized that Cabot's original cooler, a metal-lined cubicle recessed in the concrete wall, simply wouldn't be adequate to meet the needs of two people and their guests.

* * *

On this particular morning in early spring, overnight temperatures were still low and in a room shielded from warm morning sun, Cabot felt a chill settle into his elderly bones. Although he had adapted to the idiosyncrasies of his building and simply didn't pay attention to minor inconveniences, he still thought, A little heat would sure be nice.

He picked up the notebook in which he recorded each day's events and items of interest, but before he began writing, he paged through the small book of birds he kept on his kitchen table. It was one of his favorites, but it didn't have any pictures. That didn't seem right, so he had made his own sketches and inserted his illustrations between the pages of descriptions. There was one more sketch he wanted to add. Later, he thought as he scanned his notes from the day before and began to consider what he would write about this morning. He picked up his pencil, but couldn't seem to grasp it firmly. The notebook page before him seemed to blur. Never one to give up, he shook his head and struggled to focus, but the paper faded into nothingness, his pencil fell to the floor, the chill in the room enveloped him.

* * *

Flags in the city of Desert Hot Springs were flown at half mast on the day of Cabot's funeral. It seemed as if everyone in town was at the service. It was understood that an era had ended. The pueblo was unfinished as Cabot had said all along. "I will be working on expanding the building as long as I am alive." But what would become of Cabot's work now that he was no longer there to share it? Portia was not well and left to spend the last years of her life with friends.

The pueblo was abandoned. It was as if the occupants had walked out the door and never returned. No relative appeared to pack up and remove the contents of the building or even to claim it and the land it was on. It remained in its abandoned state for four years, during which time vagrants broke in and camped in it. Vandals scavenged anything they found interesting. At last the city recognized it as a problem and formulated plans to bulldoze the structures along with everything inside.

A man named Cole Eyrud had met Cabot in the early sixties and they had became fast friends. As Cole saw the destruction caused by vandalism and neglect, he tried to stop it and even asked for help in a Desert Sentinel newspaper article printed in

June of 1969. No one else seemed interested, but when he heard the city was going to destroy it all, he refused to let it happen. Whether it is true or not, the story told is that he stood in front of the building with a shotgun when the bulldozers arrived and threatened them until they turned away.

Afterwards, he found a way to buy the property and moved in with his family. However, with great respect for Cabot and Portia, the Eyrud family did not inhabit Cabot's living quarters, but lived in a separate added on apartment. He reopened the pueblo as a museum in 1970. Cole and his family lived there for the next twenty-three years, which is about the same amount of time as Cabot was there. When Cole passed away in 1996, his daughter, Trudy, gave the property and its contents to the city of Desert Hot Springs with the condition that it must be used as a museum.

In looking back over the colorful and adventurous life of Cabot Yerxa, one of the most important events was his miraculous discovery of hot water. While easily explained today by understanding earthquake faulting, it did seem like a miracle to Cabot at the time. But an almost more miraculous situation existed after his death. Considering the pueblo stood unattended and abandoned for four long years, how is it possible that so many of his belongings remained? Pottery, baskets, all sorts of artifacts could easily have been carried away or destroyed by vandals just being destructive. It's true, some things were taken and a few broken, but the majority of the pueblo's contents survived and some of the stolen items have been returned anonymously. Paintings, photographs, clothing, furniture, books and papers remain today, their values totaling millions of dollars. Cabot, himself, would no doubt call it a miracle that his pueblo and most of its contents survived the four years it sat deserted and unwanted. Miracle Hill is well-named.

COFFEE'S BATHHOUSE
Al Jolson, William Powell, William Holden

When was the last time you spent a Saturday afternoon in a "rubbing room?" Can't remember? No wonder, since in today's world it would be called a massage. But back in the 1940's when L.W. Coffee was making plans to build the biggest and best bathhouse anyone could imagine, "rubbing room" was an appropriate term. Coffee was a visionary. He saw opportunity and knew how to make it happen.

It was 1934 when Coffee began drilling his first well and from that early beginning, his plans expanded to include layout of streets, homes, businesses, electricity, postal and telephone service and most importantly, the biggest and most extensive public bathhouse anywhere in the country. In the short time span of six years, from 1941 to 1947, L.W. Coffee developed a few square miles of raw desert into the beginning of the town of Desert Hot Springs.

It was the natural hot mineral water that drew Coffee and his wife, Lilian, from their home in Los Angeles to the remote, mostly unpopulated desert site. It was the water, Coffee predicted, with its healing and restorative properties that, like a magnet, would pull people to this windswept alluvial plain on the south slope of the Little San Bernardino Mountains.

An essential part of Coffee's vision for his development was based on the idea of a public bathhouse utilizing the abundant, natural, hot mineral water readily available to anyone willing to dig a well. By 1941 the only business in town was the Idle Hour

Cafe and less than a dozen homes had been erected. But it was enough for Coffee to go ahead with plans for his bathhouse. His first attempt to provide hot baths from the naturally heated water began with one tub in a tank house. As public usage made it clear more tubs were needed, he added another one outside. It was constructed of concrete and protected with a temporary shelter. Demand increased with availability and shortly it became apparent two tubs were still insufficient to serve the public.

With typical Coffee enthusiasm, he began the creation of his dreams and by the middle of summer, he'd built the kind of bathhouse he'd always envisioned. Along with the various therapeutic pools of different temperatures, there were individual cubicles for sweat cots, a rubbing room, fountain-grill, offices and a swimming pool utilizing a continuous supply of fresh hot water.

July 12, 1941 was the big day, the official opening of Coffee's Hot Mineral Baths. The public was invited and while the population of the new town was still under 100, it was estimated that the attendance might possibly swell to as many as 250 people. Hoping for a memorable event and moving ahead with his usual optimism and flourish, Coffee prepared with 2,000 foot-long hot dogs, Parker House rolls, ice cream and soft drinks.

The festivities began at 7:00 P.M. with speeches by dignitaries including Robert Dillon, county supervisor, for whom Dillon Road was later named. By 8:00 P.M. after the pools were opened and the dance floor was crowded with people swinging to the sounds of a full orchestra, the actual count added up to over 2,000 attendees. By 11:00 P.M. the hot dogs were gone and by 1:00 A.M. the ice cream and soft drink bins were empty, but the bathers in the pools and couples swaying on the dance floor refused to leave. It was after 2:00 in the morning before the grounds were finally cleared.

No records were kept of the names of those present at this memorable event, but it's highly likely there were many celebrities mixing with ordinary people that unusual evening. One who was known to frequent the bathhouse was Al Jolson, who, according to PBS, "was the first openly Jewish man to become an entertainment star in America."

Born Asa Yoelson (1886) in Lithuania, he rose to stardom as a comedian, singer and actor. By 1920 he was the highest paid entertainer and by 1928 had over eighty hit records and sixteen national and international tours. In those days without the benefit of television, entertainers became famous by their live appearances on tours around the country.

Bob Hope may be known for his Christmas trips overseas to entertain servicemen during the war years, but it was Jolson, who, beginning right after the attack on Pearl Harbor was the first to entertain our troops in foreign countries. He was also the first to perform for U.S. Soldiers in Korea in 1950.

Those who remember Jolson often think of him for his performance in **The Jazz Singer** (1927), the first "talkie." His popularity was so great that nearly twenty years later his life was the subject of a movie, **The Jolson Story** (1946) in which he was portrayed by Larry Parks with Jolson's voice dubbed in for the musical numbers.

Jolson was white, but he not only sang black music, he often performed in blackface makeup. While this would not be acceptable today, back then it was fresh and entertaining. Jolson was the "rock star" of his time and helped pave the way for later black performers such as Louis Armstrong, Duke Ellington and Fats Waller.

William Powell who was frequently seen at Coffee's bathhouse, most likely attended its big opening night. Six years younger than Al Jolson, his early movie career was made playing the role of a villain and later, that of a detective. Beginning with silent films, his smooth voice and timing made it easy for him to move into the "talkies." With three academy award nominations, he is most often remembered as Nick Charles in *The Thin Man,* playing opposite Myrna Loy. Later after his divorce from his second wife, Carole Lombard, he starred with Jean Harlow in **Reckless** (1935) and fell madly in love with her. During their two-year engagement, she became ill and died. Powell was devastated, but eventually he put the loss behind him and married Diana Lewis, a woman he'd known only three weeks. This marriage lasted forty-four years until his death of cardiac arrest in Palm Springs in 1984. Since most of Powell's movie career took place prior to the 1940's, he would have been recognized as a well-known celebrity at Coffee's bathhouse.

William Holden, another star known to have frequented Coffee's Hot Mineral Baths, was born in 1918 making him considerably younger than both Jolson and Powell. His career in movies was just beginning during the early 1940's. At the time of the opening of the bathhouse, Holden had been in only nine of the 63 movies he acted in during his lifetime. His last film role was in 1981, the year in which he died from loss of blood after a fall.

Holden was often referred to as Hollywood's "Golden Boy," a title from the movie in which he played his first starring role in 1939. Many of his fans are more likely to recall some of his most memorable roles in movies such as **Stalag 17** (1953), **The Bridges at Toko-Ri.** (1954), **Picnic,** (1955), **Love is a Many-Splendored Thing,** (1955), **The Bridge on the River Kwai,** *(1957).*

Holden was best man at the marriage of Ronald Reagan and Nancy Davis in 1952. He received an Academy Award for best actor in **Stalag 17**, and was on the cover of **Life** magazine (1954). He received the Primetime Emmy Award for Outstanding Lead Actor for **The Blue Knight** (1974). His personal life was not always so successful. A stormy 30 year marriage to Brenda Marshall ended in divorce and Holden's alcoholism was a frequent contributor. One incident in particular occurred in Italy in 1966. While driving drunk, he caused an accident that resulted in the death of the driver of the other car.

Holden was seriously interested in wildlife preservation as well as big game hunting, a hobby he was able to pursue in Africa where he held a major interest in the Mt. Kenya Safari Club. But one resident of the desert remembers a hunting story involving Holden and a friend that was not quite what the actor expected. The incident as it was related went like this:

* * *

It was an exceptionally hot day for early Spring as the two hunters turned their Jeep off the highway onto a faint track in the sand and headed north towards the Little San Bernardino Mountains. The sun beat down on the men in their open vehicle. The armpits of Holden's safari-styled shirt were already stained with perspiration. He had dressed for the event in the same elegant manner as if he'd been heading out on a big game hunt in Kenya.

With hopes of finding an easy track, the men turned into a high-sided wash. They intended to follow it north until connecting with one of the canyons leading deeper into the mountains. That's where they had visions of finding bigger game. Mountain lions were known to frequent these canyons and if the hunters were lucky, they might surprise one curled up in the shade of a rock shelter while waiting out the midday heat.

Less than an hour into their expedition and nowhere near the mouth of any canyon, their Jeep bogged down in an area of deep, loose, extra fine sand. The more they gunned the motor to rock the vehicle out of its rut, the deeper its wheels dug in. Finally, admitting they were really stuck, Holden's friend turned off the engine and said, "Now what?"

"Damn," muttered Holden, "I thought Jeeps were supposed to plow through this kind of stuff. Been better if we'd taken horses."

Blazing sun beat down on the two hunters. Any breeze that might have given a small particle of relief from the heat was blocked by the walls of the wash. Holden's fashionable safari shirt clung to his back and beads of sweat rolled slowly down the sides of his face.

As a last resort, the two men, slipping and sliding in the loose sand of the steep gully walls, crawled up over the edge and out onto the desert floor. With nothing except small bushes and cholla cactus in view, they scoured the surrounding area for woody debris and anything they could use to jam around their mired wheels that might provide a gripping surface. Hours went by as they tossed dry brush, tumbleweeds and rocks over the side of the wash and stuffed them under the bogged down Jeep. By late afternoon with a stroke of luck, two wheels grabbed onto a sturdy dead branch and the vehicle finally pulled ahead.

The men were exhausted, dust-covered and disillusioned. At the first place where the bank was low enough, they gunned the vehicle up the side and took off across the sands where they found a faint gravel road. As they headed back to civilization looking forward to a few stiff drinks at a popular watering hole in Palm Springs, it was early evening.

A red sun surrounded by streaks of crimson and yellow hung just above the western horizon when a large jack rabbit leaped in huge bounds across the road in front of the big game hunters as if taunting them. Holden turned to his companion and said, "This was not a good day."

* * *

For L. W. Coffee, hunting was the last thing he was interested in. His goal in his own words, was "to help make Desert Hot Springs the highest type of Health Development in the world." When he set out to convince the skeptical "that Desert Hot Springs is THE place," his success came from recognizing the unlimited supply of hot curative, mineral water from wells differing in temperature from 104 to 180 degrees Fahrenheit.

Coffee was so committed to promoting the unique water that he provided, a special faucet on the drinking fountain at his Hot Mineral Baths, so that anyone desiring to take home some of the hot mineral water could help himself. The water was free and Coffee wrote that "many people take with them as much as twenty gallons or more at a time." He estimated that from three to five hundred gallons were carried away daily.

Coffee died of a stroke in 1957. His Hot Mineral Baths continued to operate until 1983 and finally in 1991, the deserted and deteriorating structure was demolished. While Coffee's bathhouse no longer exists, it is still possible to carry away its famous cold mineral water. Now it comes bottled in plastic from Mission Springs Water District and is still not for sale. The Water District gives the water away at special events and for promotional purposes. No one is allowed to bottle and profit from selling the exceptional water. Residents, however, are allowed to have their own wells with the curative hot water available for their individual home spas.

Now in the twenty-first century, Coffee's vision of a world class health resort has been only partially fulfilled. Greater Desert Hot Springs' laid back hometown atmosphere and abundance of secluded private spas continue to appeal to the famous and common folk, alike. Of the many spas in the area, most draw an international or national clientèle and shield their celebrity guests from public scrutiny. Rumor has it that Ben Affleck and Matt Damon frequent the We Care Spa. Celebrity visitors are reported at most of the other spas as well, but their visits are kept low key.

Perhaps it is a good thing development has been slow. The result is the natural hot water has not been exploited or misused and when the time is right, the kind of development Coffee envisioned will take place at a level even he couldn't have thought possible.

Truly Authentic
Cary Grant

If a newspaper reporter had covered this story, the headline might have read: "**Cabot Yerxa Runs Cary Grant Off His Property**" As unlikely as this may seem, it really did happen and here's how it came about.

During a visit by Cary Grant and his wife, Betsy Drake, to Paul Gregory and Janet Gaynor's Singing Tree Ranch, the conversation turned to Cabot's Pueblo located just a mile or two to the north.

Grant, already a star for his role in **Bringing Up Baby** (1938) with Katherine Hepburn and as a leading man in numerous subsequent movies, was a fan of Native American art and architecture. He had been to the pueblos at Taos, New Mexico and Santa Fe, so naturally he was intrigued when he heard the name, Cabot's Pueblo.

"Is this pueblo something we can go see?" Grant asked.

"Why not," Gregory answered, "We could go this afternoon. I think you would find it especially interesting to meet Cabot. He's an authentic desert pioneer."

Gregory had been introduced to Cabot Yerxa and thought Grant would enjoy visiting the crusty, desert homesteader and the exotic structure he was in the process of building out of mud bricks and scavenged materials. Cabot was used to visitors and often entertained writers and artists who sometimes stayed at the pueblo for extended periods of time. Cabot's physical appearance was that of a grub-staking, grizzled miner, but he was in fact, a learned intellectual who simply did not flaunt his knowledge.

An example of his wide variety of friends and contacts is found in a May, 1941 letter from Jack Krinder, one of the owners of the famous "21" Club in New York City. In it Krinder tells Cabot that after the war when things settle down, he and his wife may think of settling in the desert and living the ideal life Cabot has. He signed the letter, "Two Trigger" Jack, The Baron of 21.

On the afternoon when Grant and Gregory set off for Cabot's Pueblo, their wives, Janet Gaynor and Betsy Drake decided to stay behind and enjoy the afternoon at Singing Tree Ranch. Their decision was a good one since the trip did not turn out as planned.

Grant was intrigued with Yerxa's name and had to repeat it several times to say it correctly. "Is Yerxa his real name?" Grant asked. "Did you know my birth name was Archibald Alexander Leach? But when I first began working in Broadway comedies, they changed it to Cary Lockwood. Then when Paramount Pictures put me under contract, I became Cary Grant. I liked the name because the initials, C and G were the same as two big stars at the time, Clark Gable and Gary Cooper."

As Grant and Gregory talked they discovered they both had backgrounds connected to England. Gregory had grown up in London while living with his uncle and Grant was born in Bristol. Grant related that he was an only child and when he was nine, his mother was sent to a mental institution. His father simply told him she had gone on a long vacation. Grant remembered it as the beginning of a difficult time for him.

"When I was expelled from school," he told Gregory, "I joined a traveling stage troupe as a stilt walker. It was in July of 1920 that the troupe traveled to America to perform. I was 19 and will never forget being processed at Ellis Island along with the rest of the performers in our group. We had quite a tour, but when the troupe returned to England, they were without a stilt walker because I stayed in the U.S."

As Grant and Greogry bumped along dirt roads in Gregory's 1941 Ford, on their way to Cabot's pueblo, the two men traded thoughts about the movie business and current affairs. Grant told his friend how he felt about movie stars taking stands on popular issues of the day.

He said, "I'm opposed to actors taking sides in public and spouting spontaneously about love, religion or politics. We aren't experts on these subjects." Grant was careful to hold true to this position throughout his career.

When the two men pulled in and parked on the gravel in front of the eccentric structure known as Cabot's Pueblo, they could see the adobe brick building was still under construction. A row of unfinished walls on the top story stood out in jagged outline against a cloudless, turquoise sky. Old weathered lumber leaned against the far side of the building and a wheelbarrow caked with hardened clay residue sat nearby. A long-handled shovel firmly planted in a pile of fine sand with a hoe lying on the ground next to it indicated work was in progress.

Gregory and Grant sat in their car and waited for Cabot to come out and greet them. When he didn't appear, Gregory said, "Let's go see if the door is open. If it's locked, then he's not here." They got out of the car and walked up to the heavy wood plank door of the pueblo. A hand-lettered sign on the adobe wall outside stated that visitors were welcome. Next to it carved into a wide rustic board were the words:

> **"There is no place**
> **just like this place**
> **so this must be the place."**

After a good laugh, the men looked at each other and Grant said, "Well, what should we do now?" Gregory tested the rusty metal latch and to his surprise, the heavy wooden door swung open. They stepped from hot, glaring sunlight into a dim, but relatively cool anteroom. The inside walls were of raw adobe brick. An old railroad tie, a telephone pole and some heavily distressed beams supported the ceiling. Countless years of weathering in the desert gave them a patina no human hand could duplicate. Above the front door, two logs, their ends riddled with prior insect damage, served as roof rafters.

Irregularly shaped windows on opposite sides of the room were propped open providing a pleasant flow of air. "It's amazingly cool in here for such a hot day outside," Grant said. Little did they know they were experiencing the natural cooling system Cabot had devised and built into his pueblo.

Since no one appeared to greet the two men, they passed through the door straight ahead of them and entered a room set up like a museum. Shelves held Indian pottery, Navajo rugs, and primitive artifacts. Manos and matates sat on the floor, photographs and desert paintings lined the walls. Overwhelmed at what was obviously an exotic and varied collection, they stood in silent amazement until Gregory spoke.

"This collection is an art director's dream," he said, as he thought about all of the props and items he'd had to find for the many stage productions he produced around the country.

"Yes, in a way," said Grant, "But too bad it's not authentic, not the real thing, I was expecting, you know. I was thinking it was going to be a real Indian pueblo like those in Taos."

Cabot, working in the room above, heard their remarks and came storming down the stairs saying, "You've been here long enough, time for you to leave, NOW."

Cabot had no idea it was Cary Grant he was turning away. It was unlikely he'd ever seen any of Grant's movies. At that point, he was angry and didn't care who was there. He'd been insulted. After all, he escorted visitors through the pueblo every day and they loved it. His Indian artifacts were truly authentic.

Indian rugs, elaborately painted pottery, worked stone tools and wood carvings were displayed on shelves and in glass cases They were gifts from his many Native American friends, including Geronimo, and Samu, the last Chumash medicine man.

In his own way, Cabot was about as "authentic" as anyone could be, but Grant wasn't referring to Cabot, when he made his comment. He was thinking entirely of the building which was not like the Indian pueblos he'd visited in Santa Fe and Taos. Cabot didn't know that and was so offended he wasn't willing to listen to an explanation. He just wanted the two man to leave immediately. As they walked out, he slammed the door behind them and locked it.

The two men drove back to Singing Tree Ranch subdued and philosophical about their afternoon adventure.

"I apologize for getting us kicked out of the museum," Grant told Gregory. "It was my mistake, thinking it was going to be a true Indian pueblo."

"I should have explained," Gregory said, "that Cabot's building is in homage to the Indians. He respects Indians and understands their ways, so his intent is to honor their society, not copy it. He was born on an Indian reservation in the Dakotas and was the only white child growing up there. It makes sense he has a bond with them and their culture."

Grant said, "I feel pretty awful ruining our afternoon like this, I wish he'd given me a chance to explain."

"Never mind," said Gregory, "Cabot is Cabot, one of a kind. He's authentic even if his building isn't."

When they arrived back at the ranch, Molly, the housekeeper, greeted them with an announcement that dinner was ready and Janet and Betsy were anxious to hear about the trip to the pueblo.

Grant began, "Well it wasn't quite what I had expected."

Gregory laughed and said. "I should say not. It isn't every

day that Cary Grant gets run off of someone's property."

Cabot probably never knew the guest he ordered out of his pueblo that day would become one of the most popular movie stars ever. While Grant never earned an academy award for best actor, he did receive the special Academy Award for Lifetime Achievement in 1970 and was listed as the "Second Greatest Male Star of All Time" by the American Film Institute. He was granted an honorary degree by the 42nd Academy Awards "for his unique mastery of the art of screen acting with the respect and affection of his colleagues." He was given Kennedy Center Honors in 1981 and named "The Greatest Movie Star of All Time" in 2004 by *Premiere Magazine.* He acted or starred in seventy-four movies, four directed by Alfred Hitchcock.

Some of the female leads he starred with were Deborah Kerr in *An Affair to Remember* (1957), Audrey Hepburn in *Charade* (1963) as well as Marilyn Monroe, Marlene Dietrich, Mae West, Rosalind Russell, Ginger Rogers, Julie Andrews and Doris Day.

While the public knew him as the ideal leading man of the movies, his private life was less satisfying. He was married five times. His longest marriage lasted from 1949 to 1962 with Betsy Drake. It is said she introduced him to LSD which was legal at the time. Grant said the drug brought inner peace after yoga, hypnotism and mysticism failed him.

It was rumored Grant was gay or at the least, a bisexual. Nevertheless he held the position of Hollywood's top box office attraction for several decades. Ian Fleming stated he had a young Cary Grant in mind when he created James Bond and Sean Connery was selected for the first Bond movie because of his likeness to Grant. Even the Flintstones created an entertainer named, "Cary Granite."

Howard Hawks said, "Grant was so far the best that there isn't anybody to be compared with him." If Cabot had been aware of Cary Grant's talent and acclaim in the world of movies, would he still have rejected his company on that afternoon at the pueblo?

The "Singing Cowboy"
Gene Autry

The two men rode single file guiding their horses between massive boulders and around clumps of yucca and strangely-shaped Joshua trees. Late morning sun burned into their shoulders and sweat stained their shirts as they followed a meandering gravel trail across a dry stream bed. They'd spent the early hours of the day in Hidden Valley, cut off and concealed from the rest of the high desert landscape by monstrous tumbled rocks. In the old days, legend has it, rustlers favored this secret spot for hiding stolen cattle. It was 1948 and even though the area had become part of Joshua Tree National Monument, it still held the same allure of mystery and intrigue that had attracted cattle rustlers to use it as a hideout.

Young Jim Walsworth pulled his wide-brimmed hat further down on his forehead to avoid squinting into the bright sunlight. He gazed around at cholla cactus poking up between mounds of wind-sculpted stone and thought how much he liked being out horseback riding with his dad. He had no idea then that his day was going to become even more interesting later that afternoon.

After another hour in the saddle, the two hot, sweaty men followed a shallow canyon trail leading southwest and out of the Little San Bernardino Mountains of Joshua Tree to the desert below and the small town of Desert Hot Springs, They were looking forward to enjoying the soothing hot mineral waters unique to that area. Jim's father was an osteopath and firmly believed in the use of the natural hot water as therapy for healing.

* * *

Many years later, Jim Walsworth recalled that day with his father and the events at the hot water spa. He said, "Riding horseback through the town was easy, since Palm Drive, the main street, was still a gravel road as were all of the roads in the area north of Palm Springs. I can't remember the name of the spa where we stopped. It wasn't much, but the waters were a big deal. I remember there were a lot of rocks and rock walls."

Out in front, they tied their horses to a hitching rail conveniently located for guests on horseback. Inside, relaxing in one of the warm pools, Jim's dad got to talking with another man taking the waters. Jim was astonished to realize the other person was Gene Autry, one of his heroes from the western movies he enjoyed so much. Autry played the cowboy wearing a white hat, astride his horse, Champion, and always won out over the bad guys.

In the genre of musical westerns, he was known as the "Singing Cowboy." By the early 1940's, Autry had already achieved the status of fourth biggest box office movie attraction, surpassed only by Clark Gable, Spencer Tracy and Mickey Rooney.

Jim said, "My dad and Autry discovered they were both Shriners. Autry was a 33rd Degree Mason. They greeted each other with the High Noble greeting Shriners use, that sort of thing, and developed a camaraderie."

Jim was especially impressed when Autry came outside with them and spent some time admiring their horses. Autry talked about how the spa waters helped him with his back problems he said were the aftereffects of injuries he sustained while serving in the military. He was one of a long list of celebrities who put their careers on hold to serve in the armed forces during World War II.

When Autry joined the Army Air Corps, he was assigned to fly over the Himalayan Mountains, a dangerous air route called "The Hump." His duty was to deliver ammunition, fuel and arms to the China-India-Burma theater of war. After the war ended, he continued to serve by touring with a USO group in the South

Pacific before returning to the U.S. Prior to his entering the service, he was "King of the Cowboys." When he came out of the military to resume his movie career in 1946, Roy Rogers had stolen his title.

Autry would have been forty or forty-one when Jim and his dad ran into him at the spa in Desert Hot Springs. During his two years as a civilian, he had developed new ideas and began aiming his talents away from cowboy movies and in another direction. He became the first major movie star to turn his attention to television. He produced and starred in ninety-one episodes of *The Gene Autry Show* for CBS before he began producing other television series such as *Death Valley Days.* Ultimately he purchased radio and television stations and became owner of a major league baseball team.

Many years after young Jim Walsworth's accidental meeting with Gene Autry at the spa, and at a time when Walsworth had grown up and become an Orange Country Superior Court Judge, he once again had a chance meeting with Gene Autry. One evening when he walked into Paul D'Amico's restaurant and bar in Palm Springs, John Smith, the bartender nicknamed "Cowboy," greeted Walsworth with, "Hi, Judge." Walsworth returned the greeting with, "Hi, Cowboy." To the judge's surprise, a man in the front booth acknowledged the cowboy greeting and stood up to shake hands. It was Gene Autry. After some conversation, Walsworth reminded Autry of their meeting at the spa in Desert Hot Springs so many years before.

At the time of this chance meeting, Autry's name was well-known for his achievements other than his nearly 100 cowboy movies and his radio and television shows. He was owner of the California Angels American League baseball team and Vice President of the American League, a title he held until his death in 1998 at age 91. He had earned a long list of honors and rewards.

His five stars on the Hollywood Walk of Fame for Radio, Recording, Motion Pictures, Television and Live Theatre/

Performance are indications of his talent and abilities. He is the only star to be honored in all five categories. His friends were big names including Frank Sinatra, for whom Walsworth served as personal attorney.

Autry spent a lot of time in the desert, having owned a house in Palm Springs since the late 1930's. And in 1961 he purchased and renovated a Holiday Inn on East Palm Canyon Drive. When you stayed at the Gene Autry Hotel, your wake up call was a song by Autry.

Today the property is known as the Parker Palm Springs and is popular with a young crowd that may never have heard of Gene Autry, except as the name of a street. However, the Parker has preserved Autry's original residence and the rooms he named after friends and relatives. The hotel serves as a regular stop for sightseeing buses touring the Coachella Valley. Visiting tourists most likely admire Autry for his cowboy movie roles and have no idea of the huge role he played in Coachella Valley philanthropy. Over the years, the nonprofit Autry Foundation has donated more than $280 million to hospitals and charities.

An aspect of Autry that may be less known is his love for children. His widow, Jackie Autry, stated in an article in The Desert Sun newspaper, 2010, "Gene loved children. When he was on the road, he would always meet with dignitaries of the town and then go to the local children's hospital to see how he could help." In the Coachella Valley, Autry teamed with Frank Sinatra to support the Barbara Sinatra Children's Center in Rancho Mirage.

As if Autry's many achievements and legacy of over a dozen gold and platinum records were not enough, his holiday songs, *"Here Comes Santa Claus," " Peter Cottontail," and "Rudolph the Red-nosed Reindeer"* echo through every shopping mall in the country throughout the Holiday seasons. In 2009 the U.S. Postal Service honored him with a stamp along with Roy Rogers, William S. Hart and Tom Mix.

According to his widow, Autry held to the tenets of the "Code of the Cowboy" he created in 1937.

Gene Autry's Cowboy Code

1. The Cowboy must never shoot first, hit a smaller man, or take unfair advantage.
2. He must never go back on his word, or a trust confided in him.
3. He must always tell the truth.
4. He must be gentle with children, the elderly and animals.
5. He must not advocate or possess racially or religiously intolerant ideas.
6. He must help people in distress.
7. He must be a good worker.
8. He must keep himself clean in thought, speech, action and personal habits.
9. He must respect women, parents and his nation's laws.

The cowboy is a patriot.

When young Jim Walsworth first met Gene Autry at the spa in Desert Hot Springs, he knew it was a meeting worth remembering, but never could he have imagined the future celebrity status that Autry would earn and that so much of Autry's history would be preserved and available to the public through his opening of the Gene Autry Western Heritage Museum in Los Angeles. Recently the museum expanded and has become the Autry National Center featuring the history of America's West.

The Singing Cowboy left his brand on the world he portrayed in the movies and the real world in which he lived. He carried out his ideals by serving in the military during a perilous period in U.S. history and with charitable giving throughout his life.

Perhaps a New York Times review of a book, *Public Cowboy No. 1, The Life and Times of Gene Autry*, by Holly George Warren, says more about Autry than listing his achievements. "Johnny Cash called him a major influence, Ringo Starr wanted to be a cowboy like him, and Willie Nelson named a son for him."

For those who grew up during Autry's movie-making period

and remember the idealized version of life in the western deserts and plains, it may seem sad that life is so urbanized today. But for some, like Judge Walsworth, those bygone times are memories that complete one man's circle of experiences.

HENRY FORD'S MAN
Harry Bennett

In the 1950's when the Harry Bennetts were in residence just outside of Desert Hot Springs, they participated in the local social scene like any other residents. The Palm Springs Circus parade and Western Week parade that opened the season usually included a contingent of three to five horseback riders representing Bennett's S-Star Ranch. One wonders how much residents of Desert Hot Springs or Palm Springs knew about the background of the infamous Harry Bennett.

Bennett worked for Henry Ford as "his right hand man." In the 1930's and 40's he was head of Ford's Service Department or Internal Security. That really meant he did whatever Ford asked. Many of those requests involved unlawful persuasion. He handled Ford's labor relations which included intimidating workers who were talking about unionizing. Intimidation included every kind of threat, brutal beatings and a number of killings, all covered up at the time.

By the 1950's Harry Bennett was no longer working for the Ford Company and the Bennett family was spending their winters just outside of Desert Hot Springs. The local newspaper, **The Desert Sentinel,** reported events of interest and often included items involving the Harry Bennetts – visitors at their ranch, parties, dinners and teas at which they entertained. In the June 15, 1950 edition, it was reported the Bennett family left for their farm in Michigan and would return in September. Which they did and also brought along a new pet raccoon they'd acquired over the summer. But earlier that same year in April a different kind of headline and news story hit the paper.

Harry Bennett Seriously Injured in Auto Accident on Dillon Road.

There have been many Sundays when Harry Bennett has entertained his guests at his beautiful home on a high elevation at his S-Star Ranch but last Sunday Mr. Bennett spent a quiet day with his family. He and Dale Morris, who has charge of the ranch drove to Palm Springs. They were returning home about 4:30 P.M.

The article goes on to say the accelerator stuck and as Dale reached down to release it, the car struck a rock in the road causing a blowout, which threw it out of control. The car rolled over several times. Harry Bennett sustained several broken ribs, internal injuries and a concussion. Dale suffered a fractured skull and was in serious condition. The badly damaged car was a month old Cadillac. Apparently, at that time, Harry didn't feel any loyalty to Ford cars.

The article goes on to describe Harry Bennett as Henry Ford's right hand man who was instrumental in improving labor conditions by voluntarily raising employees' pay at the Ford factory to $5 a day, which at the time was the highest pay for labor anywhere in the country. Was the newspaper sugar coating their infamous resident or did the reporter really not know of Bennett's more notorious reputation?

It is interesting to note that for all of the thirty years he worked for Henry Ford and even after he was fired and retired to the desert, Bennett was surrounded by bodyguards. His winter home off Dillon Road just three miles from Desert Hot Springs included armed guards and dogs. The ranch house was built on the side of a hill with panoramic views in every direction. No one could sneak up close to the house without being seen. Bennett is said to have sometimes fired shots into the air which could be heard from far away and when he played his organ, one of his hobbies, the music filled the pure desert air and carried over the valley for miles.

Bennett's other homes in the Midwest were built with secret escape tunnels, bright lights, locked gates and every precaution he could think of. His Lodge on Lost Lake in Michigan even included pointed stakes in its surrounding lagoon. Yet, it took a simple auto accident to give him the injuries many would have liked to inflict on him.

A few months later *The Desert Sentinel* featured another article involving the Bennetts. In a picture of the local sixth grade graduating class, Esther Bennett, Harry's daughter, was lauded as the outstanding student in the small class of six.

Over sixty years later, a woman living in Palm Desert recalls attending seventh and eighth grades at the Nelly Coffman School in Palm Springs with the Bennetts' daughter. Their friendship blossomed and many good times were spent at the Bennett home, often riding horses around their ranch. Along with Esther, she also rode one of the Bennetts' S-Star Ranch horses in the Palm Springs parades. She recalls Harry Bennett as heavy set, of medium height and very nice. She often had dinner at their house.

She remembers being picked up and taken to the ranch since Esther was never allowed to go alone to anyone's home. Then one day when the car from Esther's house came to get her, the driver got out, walked around the front of the car and stood next to the front wheel. His jacket fell open as he leaned back. Her mother saw the gun in its leather holster at his side. That was the end of her visits to the Bennett house. Her mother would never let her go there again.

"This was a period of time," she said, "when it was common knowledge mobsters were visitors and even residents of Palm Springs. They were seen in restaurants and bars with influential people. Everyone just accepted it and paid little attention. Usually they were easy to recognize due to their dress and manner. Mr. Bennett had a presence about him," she said. She had no recollection of Mrs. Bennett, Esther's mother.

Bennett's presence made itself known throughout his life. It began with a street brawl when he was a sailor just off a ship. An acquaintance of Henry Ford witnessed the fight and was so impressed with the way the young sailor handled himself that he convinced the police it wasn't Bennett's fault and saved him from going to jail. The friend was on his way to a meeting with Henry Ford and decided to take the young tough along. Ford was intrigued with the sailor and offered him a security job at the Ford Motor plant. Rumor has it that Ford had only one question for the new recruit. "Can you shoot?"

Bennett quickly assembled a gang of wrestlers, boxers, football players and Detroit river gang members as Service Department employees. From then on it was simply a matter of carrying out any order Henry Ford gave him.

The most notorious of Bennett's schemes to satisfy Ford was probably The Battle of the Overpass. On May 26, 1937, union sympathizers gathered to distribute handbills on an overpass to one of the Ford Company's gates. Walter Reuther and Richard Frankensteen were there along with others to hand out material on unionizing. Bennett's goons trapped them in the center of the overpass and began beating up everyone including women. Reporters had gathered for the event and took pictures, but Bennett's thugs turned on the reporters as soon as they finished with the organizers. The reporters were assaulted and their cameras smashed. But one cameraman was able to drop his camera into a convertible under the overpass. It was quickly spirited away and the pictures of the shocking event were published in the next day's papers. The horrendous tactics of Harry Bennett carrying out Henry Ford's orders were there for the world to see.

The murder of Lewis Bradford was, after The Battle of the Overpass, the next most widely known of Bennett's iron fist methods. Bradford died on November 30, 1937, from a skull fracture occurring inside the River Rouge Plant. The Ford Motor

Company claimed it was an accident and told the family to leave town and not ask any questions. The obituary writer was twice brought before Bennett and told what and how to write the article for the newspaper. Two revolvers sat on the desk as Bennett dictated the wording to be used. Bradford's sin was being on the side of labor in the 1930's as workers tried to unionize.

Bradford, a Methodist minister, worked on the Ford Motor Company assembly line for eighteen months in 1936-37. During that time Bennett organized shameless acts of terrorism to keep workers from organizing. Bradford had an influential radio show and was gaining success in informing the public and gathering support for labor.

Meanwhile Ford sympathized with Adolph Hitler and was giving money to support him. Their bond was such that Hitler even had a photograph of Ford on display in his office. In the end Ford and Bennett were able to defeat all labor candidates in the election even though it took murder and beatings to do it. A New York Times article reported there had been 900 arrests of union sympathizers in the city of Dearborn, alone. Bribing policemen to keep the law on Ford's side was routine.

Only those who lived through this tumultuous time know the true intimidation tactics used by Bennett to stop the United Auto Workers from gaining control. It has been reported that Hitler's Gestapo was modeled on the tactics of Bennett at the Ford Motor Company.

When Bennett's career as a tough guy willing to go to any means to satisfy Henry Ford's desires, came to an end, the reward he'd been promised never materialized. Edsel Ford, Henry's son, held the Ford Company presidency for a short time, but his views differed so drastically from his father's that some sources say Henry had him killed. There is no information to confirm whether Bennett had a hand in the event. Ford who had promised Bennett the presidency after Edsel, made no attempt to follow through when his grandson, Henry Ford II, took over and fired Bennett.

It was 1945 when Bennett spent the afternoon destroying all of his files and records before he left the Ford Company after thirty years of service. When Henry Ford, Sr. was informed of the firing, he supposedly said in the most casual manner, "Well now, Harry is back on the streets where he started."

But Harry wasn't really back on the streets. Instead, he retreated to his country home and left the Midwest during the cold winter months. By settling on a remote ranch in the California desert, as far away from Detroit as possible, he sought respectability in a small town. With contracts out on his life, he had to be careful, but in the isolated desert east of Desert Hot Springs, he could have his body guards and live a fairly normal life. Of the mobsters who frequented Palm Springs, Bennett was far less recognizable than most. Basking in the winter desert sun, tending to his horses at the S-Star Ranch surrounded by untamed desert and retiring to the family's ranch in Michigan when the weather turned uncomfortably hot seemed to work pretty well for Henry Ford's former enforcer.

Were the residents of Desert Hot Springs aware of Bennett's previous life? Probably not and even if some of them did know, the desert was a "live and let live" type of place. Harry Bennett died in 1979 of natural causes.

SCANDAL IN THE DUNES
Jennifer Jones

Young Dick Roger was spending another summer with his grandparents, owners of the B-Bar-H Ranch, where celebrities came to stay and play. It was 1950 and Dick was eleven years old. Girlfriends and sex were not yet a part of his life. He was just a kid riding his horse, Arky, around the ranch and out into the desert. Having shown himself to be responsible although somewhat reckless, his grandfather, Jay Kasler, gave him free rein, just like Dick gave the horse he rode. He was allowed to spend his days doing whatever eleven year old boys liked to do. Dick liked to ride his horse and explore Seven Palms Valley where the ranch was located.

There wasn't much nearby except for a few other ranches within easy riding distance. Otherwise it was sand dunes, shallow dry washes and a few clumps of tamarisk trees that provided shade and a secluded place to hang out. The town of Desert Hot Springs to the north was just beginning to develop. Streets had been laid out and the main artery, Palm Drive, boasted a few businesses run by adventurous entrepreneurs.

* * *

When Dick saddled Arky one Saturday morning and took off for a ride, he avoided the newly emerging town and headed out into barren desert, where the wind piled tiny grains of quartz sand into dunes the size of rolling hills.

After prowling around a tamarisk grove and some shallow

washes south of the ranch, and finding nothing particularly interesting, he headed back to the B-Bar-H. It was lunch time and he pictured the ranch guests lined up at the buffet, filling their plates with salads and sandwiches before heading outside to their favorite tables near the pool.

With only a short distance to go before he arrived back at the stables, he urged Arky up a small rise. His eye caught a glimpse of something bright red and yellow, colors unnatural to the desert terrain. A slight pressure on Arky's reins turned the horse in the direction of the strange sight. Moving to the ridge of the next dune put young Dick close enough to make out the form of a person stretched out on a brightly colored blanket. He was still too far away to see clearly and just as he was about to ride Arky over to investigate, he realized the person was naked, a woman lying on her stomach. He wanted to get closer to make sure she was not in trouble, yet caution and a reluctance to approach a completely undressed female scared him. As he tried to decide what to do, the woman moved her arms and readjusted her position on the blanket.

The eleven-year old, carefully backed up his horse and, when out of sight, turned Arky and headed back to the ranch. As he rode the short distance to the corral, his mind working overtime at the sight of a woman without any clothes, he thought about a conversation he'd heard and remembered because it seemed pretty daring. Two guests the day before were complimenting a tall dark-haired woman on her fantastic suntan.

"Jennifer, how do you get such an even tan without any strap marks from your bathing suit?"

She laughed. "It's easy, I walk out to a low place in the dunes and take off my swim suit when I sunbathe." A shocked silence followed before the group of three burst into hearty laughter.

Dick realized then the naked person must be Jennifer in her secret tanning spot. He blushed thinking how embarrassed he would have been had he ridden over to her. But he couldn't get the sight of that woman without clothes out of his mind. At eleven years old, nude women were not on his list of experiences. What would she look like up close? Would any of her "private parts" be showing? Excitement began to build in his mind even as the fear of getting caught doing something he shouldn't lurked in the back of his brain.

Back at the ranch, after unsaddling Arky and sending him into the paddock with the other horses, Dick forgot about the lunch he'd been anticipating and turned casually in case anyone should notice him, to walk purposefully, as if he were on an errand. When out of eyesight from the horse corral, he followed Arky's tracks back to where he had seen the sunbather. His heart was beating so fast he could hear it. He was going to get up close and spy on a naked woman. It wasn't right, he knew, yet, he trudged on, At the base of a small dune he stopped, crept on all fours, then scrunched up the sloping rise on his stomach and elbows. He was almost afraid to lift his head the few inches necessary to peek over the top. What if she was looking his way and saw him? But having gone this far there was no going back without a glimpse of the nakedness he knew lay just a short distance on the other side of the mound.

He raised his head just enough to peek over the built-up edge of fine sand and pebbles and there she was, all tan, smooth skin, feet aimed in his direction, arms bent at the elbows, making a v-shaped frame for her head of dark flowing hair. The rise of her hips and bare bottom in plain sight sent a shiver down his spine. The blanket beneath her could have been any color in the world because he couldn't take his eyes off her body. As he watched, she raised her head and glanced sideways. He ducked down, his heart beating out of his chest. Had she seen him?

Not daring to stay longer, and fearful of being found out, he lowered his head and slowly slid on his stomach backwards down the sandy slope. When he was well enough hidden, he stood up, shook the sand out of his shirt and hurried back to the ranch. He *picked up his plate in the kitchen, filled it with items from the dining room buffet and took it out behind the tack shed to eat by himself and savor his morning adventure.*

* * *

Jennifer Jones never knew she'd been spied upon by an innocent eleven year old boy. Nor did the young boy realize the woman he had viewed naked was a famous movie star who seven years earlier had already won an Academy Award for best actress. She played a nun in **The Song of Bernadette** (1943) and was nominated for best actress. Ingrid Bergman was nominated the same year for her role in **For Whom the Bell Tolls.** Jones assumed the award would go to Bergman and when it was awarded to her, she actually apologized to Bergman for winning the Oscar.

But Bergman told her, "You were better than I was, you deserved it."

Greer Garson, the winner for **Mrs. Miniver** the year before, presented the Oscar to Jones. The next year Jones was the presenter who handed the award to Bergman for her role in **Gaslight.** Jones was nominated as Best Actress four more times during her career, which ended in 1974 with **The Towering Inferno.**

Jennifer Jones was born Phyllis Isley in 1919. Her parents owned and performed in a tent show theatrical group that toured the Midwest. Phyllis spent a year at Northwestern University after which she attended the American Academy of Dramatic Arts and met Robert Walker, who also became a star. They married in 1939 and pursued their acting careers together. After the births of two sons and a series of lean years in getting roles they moved to Hollywood in 1941, where David O. Selznick put Phyllis under contract.

It was Selznick who "discovered" Phyllis Isley in the 1930's when she was a John Robert Powers model and changed her name to Jennifer Jones. He began casting her in movies and her career took off.

Selznick's wife left him in 1945 due to his affair with Jones. In the same year Jones and Walker, who had been separated since 1943, finalized their divorce. Walker who played the villain in Alfred Hitchcock's *Strangers on a Train* died six years later (1951) at age 32. The emotional problems and drinking that plagued him, he attributed to the loss of his wife.

Jones, under the direction of Selznick played in major movies including *Duel in the Sun* (1946) and *Portrait of Jennie* (1948). In 1949 she and Selznick married, a union that lasted for fifteen years until his death in 1965. Their marriage was marred by the tragic death of their only daughter, Mary Jennifer. She committed suicide by jumping from a twenty-two story building in Los Angeles.

Young Dick Roger visiting his grandparents on their ranch in the desert didn't go to a lot of movies and those he did see were mainly westerns, so he had little interest in the movie stars who came to the B-Bar-H. But because of his boyhood spying adventure, he never forgot Jennifer Jones. Four years later in June of 1954 when *Indiscretion of an American Wife* starring her and Montgomery Clift was playing at the new Desert Hot Springs Theater, Dick who was now fifteen and using his given name, Richard, made sure he went to the movie. In fact, he took his girlfriend, Marcia Kane and in the dark of the theater, he experienced his first kiss. But it wasn't Marcia, Richard was thinking of when their lips met, it was the raven-haired beauty on the silver screen who occupied his thoughts.

Jennifer Jones with twenty-five movies to her credit, was still starring in films in 1971 when she met Norton Simon, the wealthy industrialist. She became his wife for twenty-two years until he passed away in 1993. Simon spent more than 100 million on his art collection housed in the Norton Simon Museum in Pasadena, California. Jones served as chairwoman of the museum until she passed away in 2009 at age ninety.

As for young Dick Roger, he grew up loving the desert and, after medical school, returned to the Coachella Valley to practice cardiology. For twenty-five years he served as Chief of Cardiology at Eisenhower Medical Center and Hospital in Palm Desert. He treated numerous stars and celebrities, some of whom he says "forgot" to pay him or simply couldn't be bothered with details such as paying bills.

Roger's home in Palm Desert is filled with mementos of early California ranch life. Wooden beams, tile floors, all of the architectural elements of the adobe style, contribute to an authentic setting for someone with Roger's experience. His love of horses has stayed with him and one of his favorite activities is going on long trail rides with groups of other horsemen. Roger's formative years at the B-Bar-H Ranch and the landscape he loved have remained important to him, not just as memories of the past, but as a way of life in the desert.

A Pink Dress and Red Shoes
Mamie Eisenhower

After his term in office, President Dwight D. Eisenhower and his wife, Mamie, stayed at the El Dorado Country Club in Palm Desert for three months out of the year. Mamie often had time on her hands and when writer and journalist, Glory Munday Hartley, invited her to go shopping or out to lunch, Mamie happily accepted. On one of those occasions, as a topic of conversation, Glory thought Mrs. Eisenhower would find it interesting to hear about the good work going on at Angel View, a crippled children's hospital in Desert Hot Springs. Glory's son, Danny Munday, was at Angel View, so she could speak from personal experience. Danny had been afflicted with polio and Glory had taken him to Angel View in the 1950's. Her firsthand experience at the hospital impressed Mrs. Eisenhower and she wanted to know more about this facility that was changing the lives of crippled children. Glory couldn't resist telling her a story about the Hortons, friends of hers, who owned the grocery store in Desert Hot Springs.

It was during a time when money for charities was often difficult to raise. Alan Horton was impressed with the caring, healing work taking place at Angel View and he tried to help out as much as he could, doing odd jobs and minor repairs, He became acquainted with many of the severely disabled children unable to walk or even feed themselves. Yet after treatments in the natural, mineral-laden, hot water, therapeutic baths, their mobility was restored. Alan was impressed. He wanted to do more.

He knew money at the hospital was in short supply, so he made an arrangement with Mody, the cook at the children's home, to select whatever she needed at his grocery store, Horton's, and put it on their tab instead of bringing money to pay each time. Mody was happy because this was much easier for her and allowed her to shop for nutritious foods for the disabled children without worrying so much about the cost. This arrangement continued for months and finally at the end of the year, Alan sent Angel View a bill for the food. Across the bottom and next to the totaled amount, written in big red letters were the words, **Paid in Full.**

After listening to Glory's story of Alan's generosity, Mrs. Eisenhower sat quietly and thought for a moment before she said, "I'd like to meet Mr. Horton." Glory was more than happy to make that happen and promised Mamie a trip to Desert Hot Springs.

A few days later, Mamie and two secret service men pulled up in front of Horton's grocery store. One of the security men got out of the serious-looking black car and entered the front door of Horton's store. He walked up to a clerk and politely asked if Mr. Horton could be summoned and would he please come outside at the request of Mrs. Eisenhower.

Raye, Alan's wife, remembers the event distinctly, because Alan had been working at the vegetable bins and was wearing his work apron. He was so shocked to be told the president's wife was asking to meet him, that he couldn't stop to think, he just marched out the front door and didn't even remember he was wearing the disgustingly stained apron that he used to keep his clothes clean as he sorted, trimmed and rearranged vegetables in his produce section.

"He was really embarrassed," Raye said. "He felt he should have removed his apron as a sign of respect. But he was so taken by surprise, he didn't even think of it. I couldn't blame him. After all we'd never had a United States President's wife stopping by our store before."

After her introduction to the Hortons, Mamie wanted to know how Angel View came by its name. Glory began by pointing out the angel-shaped rock formation on the side of Mt. San Jacinto. "This angel-in-the-mountain was the inspiration for the name, Angel View," she said. "Because of its location, the white rocks forming the shape of an angel with outstretched wings can only be seen from Desert Hot Springs."

Dr. Robert Bingham was the first to introduce disabled children to the healing waters of the desert. He was the originator of the hospital and donated the land from which the angel on the mountain can be seen. The idea of an angel as a symbol of hope for disabled children caught on and the name, Angel View, used not only for the hospital, but for its string of resale shops throughout the Coachella Valley continues to this day.

Glory, with her zeal to promote the children's hospital, got the idea that even though Alan Horton did a lot for Angel View, his wife, Raye, could help raise funds by putting on a luncheon. If Mamie Eisenhower would agree to be their special guest, she thought they could raise a large amount of money. When Glory called Mamie to invite her, she said she would be happy to attend.

Raye took a deep breath and began planning for the big event. She figured out if she used her dining room and moved all of her furniture out of the living room and den, she would have enough space to seat sixty people at small tables. Horton's Grocery Store would donate the food and each guest would be charged $5.00, all to be donated to Angel View.

Over fifty years later Raye's friend, Virginia Jacobson, recalled the day of the luncheon.

"I specifically remembered how much I loved your beet salad," she said to Raye. Raye looked at her and raised an eyebrow, "It wasn't a beet salad, it was a beet mold with horseradish sauce. I also served a crab salad and marinated green beans. I don't remember what else. What I do remember is I got cold feet several days before the luncheon. I got to thinking, *How can I get out of this? I can't handle this many people.* Fortunately there was a very nice restaurant in town run by Chuck Hayden, Sr. His son still lives in town, but the restaurant is no longer there. Anyway, I went to him and begged. He agreed to help by bringing several of his waitresses to put the plates of food together in the kitchen, to serve and clean up. He also supplied china, silver, glassware and serving utensils to all of the tables except Mamie's. I put her in the dining room with my best china and silver. The plates had flowers that looked nice on my favorite damask table cloth. All of the other tables were covered with plain white cloths and white plates from Hayden's restaurant."

Virginia thought for a moment and said, "Remember the dozens and dozens of pink and red paper carnations we made? We scattered them on the white tables and it was really pretty. Afterward we used them for other events and even made more. Remember when we completely covered Minnas' car with them for a parade. Minnas was a favorite dress shop in town. We all bought clothes there."

Raye recalled the day of the luncheon, "Mamie arrived wearing red shoes and a pink flowered dress. When some of the ladies complimented her on her dress, she told us a story about herself. 'As I was getting dressed,' she said, 'my maid told me emphatically, Surely you aren't going to wear red shoes with that pink dress, are you? Well, I looked her squarely in the eye and said, I certainly am!' The story set everyone at ease."

At the end of the luncheon, Mamie went out to the patio to take in the expansive view of creosote-covered dunes rolling up to the foot of majestic Mt. San Jacinto in the distance. She wanted to see if the angel on the mountain could be seen from Raye's house. The white-winged image showed clearly through the pure desert air, but Mamie didn't have a lot of time to savor the view. Even though most of the guests had greeted her with a handshake and "Hello, how nice of you to come," when she first arrived, they couldn't resist following her to the patio. Admiring women clustered around the former first lady for more conversation and more compliments on her lovely pink dress and red shoes. They were having such a good time, no one left until long after the secret service men escorted Mamie to her waiting car.

It was then that Raye, still excited, but rapidly wilting, dropped into the nearest chair and announced, "We did it, the first lady of the United States came to lunch in Desert Hot Springs."

The Eisenhowers continued to take an interest in Angel View and attended benefits and fund raising events to support the hospital. But it is Glory Munday Hartley who deserves a place in history for having introduced the Eisenhowers to Desert Hot Springs and the crippled children's facility that has made a difference in the lives of so many young people.

There was a lot of talk that year in Desert Hot Springs about the enormously successful luncheon for Mamie Eisenhower that Raye Horton hosted at her home. But equally recognized that spring was the most fashionable outfit seen around town, a pink dress with red shoes.

HARDWARE AND HORSES
Elizabeth Taylor, John Travolta

As an eleven year old boy, Jim Haidet always looked forward to spending some of his free time at the B-Bar-H Ranch where his mother, Ruth, worked. She helped out at the popular dude ranch whenever a need existed and frequently that involved doing a favor for one of their celebrity guests. As an adolescent boy, Haidet was too busy growing up and pursuing his own interests to pay much attention to the famous guests his mother met during her working hours. He does, however, remember one time at the dinner table when she casually commented that she'd spent the afternoon sewing some buttons on a shirt for Peter Lorre. The name was one of the few familiar to Haidet who had seen Lorre numerous times at the dude ranch's horse corral.

"He was a frequent visitor at the B-Bar-H Ranch," Haidet said. "Because my mother worked there, I was allowed to ride the horses in exchange for doing some chores in the stables. While I didn't pay much attention to the celebrities staying there, I knew Peter Lorre because he was a good rider and I respected his way with horses."

One day at the stables, when Haidet was pitching hay and helping to clean horse stalls, a beautiful young girl with creamy white skin and jet black hair came into the shed. She asked to have a horse saddled up for an afternoon ride. As Haidet stood, speechless and tongue tied, an older stable hand poked him to get his attention. "That there's Elizabeth Taylor, he whispered.

You know, that young girl in the movie, *National Velvet.* It's playing right now in a lot of theaters." Haidet hadn't been to a lot of movies, but he made up his mind right then that he would see National Velvet. The movie debued in 1944 and also starred Mickey Rooney and Angela Lansbury. While generally reliable, on this day, he remembers being so impressed with the presence of a movie star so close to his own age and so outstandingly beautiful, he could hardly do anything right. It was a day he'd never forget.

The Haidet family had moved to Desert Hot Springs in the early 1940's when Dillon Road was still called Aqueduct Road and the only light in town after dark was at the Idle Hour Cafe on Palm Drive. The move was decided during a brief visit when Jim's dad who suffered from severe asthma announced it was the first time in many years he had been able to sleep all night without interruption. "We're moving to Desert Hot Springs." He announced to his family. "I don't care that there aren't any paved streets or other services. I can sleep there; it will be healthy for all of us."

They settled on 7th street and Mr. Haidet was certainly right about the health aspect of the area. L.W. Coffee's bathhouse and health spa was built just a few blocks from where the Haidets settled. An additional benefit came about when the Haidets bought a lot in Coffee's new subdivision. The purchase gave them free admission to Coffee's baths and swimming pool. While the town didn't have a fire department, the closest was Cathedral City, nor did it have a post office, sewers, street lights, city services, or much of anything, it did have the finest swimming pool and health spa anyone could imagine.

A small airstrip at Garnet served private planes delivering wealthy people to the desert playground, as well as functioning as a freight depot and post office. The desert seemed like a pretty good place to the Haidet family.

Since young Jim Haidet grew up during a time when famous guests were the norm at the B-Bar-H Ranch, he was used to celebrities and never paid much attention to the ones who showed up in town. Usually they were "old" people, probably at least in their twenties or thirties and not anyone he cared about. That changed somewhat when he went to high school in Palm Springs. Since Desert Hot Springs only had a grade school, when he began 7th grade, he and any others his age had to be bused to Palm Springs. The bus was a Model A Ford usually driven by Bill Tarbuton's wife. On good days the commute was okay, but there were times when getting to classes was a real adventure. Windstorms blew drifting sand across the road creating berms that could stop a truck, but usually the sturdy Model A was able to plow through. But there were times when the students had to get out and push. Over fifty years later, arriving in class covered with dust and grit is still fresh in Haidet's memory.

He also remembers that one of the perks in attending Palm Springs High School was that Bob Hope put on two shows every season for the school kids. Hope brought professional Hollywood entertainers to the students. Haidet can't name any of the other performers because he simply wasn't as interested in celebrities as he was in horses and sports. He just remembers how much fun the shows were with Hope as the comedian and emcee.

After high school, Haidet joined the army and served in the army ordinance corps, where he worked on maintaining surface to air missiles and Nike radar. Later he joined Motorola in its research department. Little did he dream at that time, he would return to the desert and become involved with nuts and bolts and hardware at the store opened by his father in 1945. Over sixty-five years later, Lowe's and Home Depot may have taken over in other cities, but Haidet's Hardware still serves customers in Desert Hot Springs.

Jim Haidet thinks of himself as a regular hardworking guy,

but he's had some extraordinary experiences he tends to treat casually. He never thought much about the guy wearing jeans and a tee shirt who would stop by his house to shoot baskets on the back patio. "John Travolta," Haidet said, "was just like any other guy except that he sometimes showed up wearing boots which didn't help his mobility on the court." Travolta also became interested in the model airplanes Haidet was building and sometimes they would go to Demuth Park in Palm Springs to fly models. At other times they went all the way to the polo fields in Indio. This was long before Travolta got his pilots license to fly real airplanes.

At the same time the Haidet family came to Desert Hot Springs in the early 1940's, Cabot Yerxa had arrived back in town and was busy building his exotic pueblo. Haidet remembers Cabot very well. He and his wife attended many sunrise services on Miracle Hill at Cabot's Eagle's Nest. Considering the different philosophies and religious doctrines Cabot and Portia pursued, sunrise services on Miracle Hill fit in nicely with the rest of their activities

Haidet likes to tell the story of Cabot and his snake bite remedy. He was curious what Cabot would do if one of the rattlesnakes he kept on the property happened to bite him. Most people stay away from snakes, but Cabot's burglar alarm system was unique and as usual he was using natural items close at hand. In this case it was rattlesnakes. If he was going to be away for any length of time, he put his most valuable possessions in the pueblo room with the dirt floor. Then he'd gather some of the rattlesnakes from his outside snake pit and let them loose in the room with his treasured belongings. It was common knowledge in town that he used the snakes for protection against burglary. What was not common knowledge was the number of snakes let loose each time. So even if an unscrupulous person thought they could catch or kill the guard snakes, they could never be certain there wasn't one more lurking in a crevice or corner or behind books on a shelf. The snake protection system was very effective.

In conversation one day, Haidet asked Cabot, "With all those snakes and your handling of them, isn't it likely you're going to be bitten some time? What would you do then?"

"Of course I've had snake bites," answered Cabot, "but I just lie down in my nice little sleeping cubicle and take a two hour nap. By the time I wake up I'm fine."

This may have worked for Cabot, but it is not recommended for anyone else with a snake bite. It is quite possible that Cabot's snakes did not inject venom if one of them chomped down on his arm or leg. The snakes were used to him, he fed them, kept them warm when it rained and in general took care of them. Snakes release venom only when they feel cornered and have to defend themselves. If Cabot's snakes bit him, it may have been more of an annoyed reaction rather than a fight for life.

Cabot and his snakes is just one of the many stories Jim Haidet remembers after so many years in a small town where everyone knew everyone else. Haidet was involved with Little League teams, and anything else going on. That was how he met John Santucci in 1960 when they both were volunteer fire fighters. Santucci was running a laundromat at the corner of Palm Drive and Buena Vista Ave. In time he converted the laundromat into the Capri Restaurant which was owned and operated entirely by the Santucci family until 2012. During those years, they served Italian food and steaks to a clientèle including a long list of celebrities the Santuccis' mention only if asked.

Most towns have a few families that settled there in the early days and remained a presence through several generations. The Haidets are one of those along with the Edwards, Santuccis, Morgans, Haydens and Cabot Yerxa. All of these families as well as others contributed to the growth and history of that sprawling desert landscape located just ten miles north of Palm Springs. Remembrances of celebrities reside in their everyday experiences. Each tidbit of information places another image of the small desert town on the collective mural of memory, which continues to be drawn, redrawn and expanded over the years.

View of Mt. San Jacinto from Two Bunch Palms (1937)
Courtesy of Desert Hot Springs Historical Society

Early building at Two Bunch Palms Spa (1948)
Courtesy of Sidewinder Restaurant

B-Bar-H Ranch 1941 Ford station wagon used for picking up guests at Garnet Railroad Station
Desert Hot Springs Historical Society

Peter Lorre under the B-Bar-H Ranch sign (1940's)
Courtesy of Dr. Richard Rogers

DESERT

HOT SPRINGS

California

AN ALL YEAR CLIMATE
HOT MINERAL WATERS

Coffee's Bathhouse (1950's)
Desert Hot Springs Historical Society

Eagle's Nest, Miracle Hill, first home of Cabot Yerxa (early 1940's)
Desert Hot Springs Historical Society

Cabot's Pueblo Museum, placed on National Register of Historic Places in 2012
Photo by Tom Scott

Golden Saddle dining room and pool
at B-Bar-H Ranch (1940's and '50's)
Desert Hot Springs Historical Society

Idle Hour Cafe on Palm Drive near Coffee's Bathhouse (early 1940's)
Desert Hot Springs Historical Society

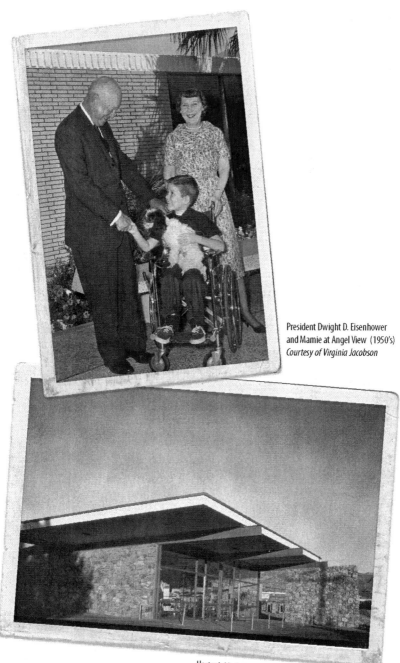

President Dwight D. Eisenhower
and Mamie at Angel View (1950's)
Courtesy of Virginia Jacobson

Horton's Market visited by Mamie Eisenhower (1955)
Courtesy Desert Hot Springs Historical Society

Paul Gregory and Janet Gaynor at Singing Tree Ranch (1960's)
Courtesy of Paul Gregory

Capri Restaurant on Palm Drive (1980's)
Courtesy Julia Santucci

GROUNDBREAKERS—Clark Gable, Mrs. A. L. Eaton, public relations director, Angel View Foundation; Mrs. N. A. Bertram, chairman of the board; Mrs. Clark Gable, and Nickey Williams, patient at AVCC, greet large crowd at hospital wing groundbreaking ceremonies. Mr. and Mrs. Gable arrived at scene in Desert Hot Springs after flying here by helicopter with Sonja Henie, Ray Ryan and others.

Character actor, Marc Lawrence
Courtesy of Julia Santucci

Remains of stone building, on Varner Road. Main stop for travelers through the Coachella Valley prior to the 1-10 Frwy.

Photo taken in 2008 by Tom Scott

Furbee's drug store on Palm Drive, filming site in Robert Altman's movie, 3 Women (1970's)
Courtesy of John Furbee

Public telephone on corner of Palm Drive and Pierson, originally located inside Furbee's drug store
Photo taken in 2010 by Nancy Cain

Program for festival at the Beat Hotel (2006)
Courtesy of the late Steve Lowe

Martha Stewart
at Sidewinder Restaurant
on Pierson Ave. (2010)
*Photo snapped by Audrey Moe
with Steven Schick's camera*

Wisteria chair made for playwright,
Tennessee Williams by designer,
Charles Hollis Jones (1960's)
Courtesy of Charles Hollis Jones

"A Living Treasure," Paul Gregory at
Historical Society Soup Supper (2012)
Photo by Bruce Montgomery

Marilyn's Retreat
Marilyn Monroe

While Singing Tree Ranch on the outskirts of Desert Hot Springs was well established as a destination for friends of Janet Gaynor and Paul Gregory, they were surprised one day by a phone call from someone they did not know well.

Molly, the housekeeper, answered the phone in the hallway and listened for a moment before handing the receiver to Janet as she said, "Marilyn Monroe would like to talk to you." Janet, the first woman to be given an Academy Award, was accustomed to calls from their many other celebrity friends in show business who came to spend time at their ranch in the desert. Since Singing Tree was a private home and not a dude ranch like the B-Bar-H, just a few miles away, it was not open to the public. Marilyn Monroe was not one of their personal friends and Janet wondered about the purpose of Marilyn's call, as she took the phone receiver from Molly and said, "Hello, this is Janet."

Marilyn's plaintive voice came right to the point, "I heard you live where there aren't many people. Could I come out and visit for a day or two?"

Janet, gracious as always, replied, "Of course you can. I'll have the guest house ready as soon as you want to come."

"Thank you," replied Marilyn, "I'll be there tomorrow. But I'll only stay for a day, maybe two, if I can arrange it."

Marilyn stayed for a week and was reluctant to leave even then. But the time finally came when she could no longer hide in the serene desert away from her admirers and the photographers who followed her everywhere.

Most of her time at Singing Tree Ranch, she spent in the guest house, alone, being herself instead of the sex idol of the country. But at times she did wander out to view ranch activities.

On one of those days, she followed Paul Gregory to the pigeon lofts as he went to attend to the 5,000 pair of Marseille Mondain Pigeons he raised and sold to restaurants that served squab as one of their specialty dishes.

The birds were housed in six lofts, each 150-200 feet long. The lofts were set twelve to fifteen feet apart so the tractor used for delivering food and water as well as hauling away droppings could be driven between them. In the front of each loft was a fly space, so the birds could flutter about. While Paul filled feeding trays and added fresh water to the drinking cups, he explained to Marilyn how the birds were taken care of and how the fence surrounding the lofts kept out coyotes. "Coyotes would love to raid the hen house," he told her, "And not only coyotes, but cougars come up the wash and stand on the bank practically licking their lips as they think about getting at these birds."

Marilyn gazed quietly at the pigeons as they stirred about, ruffling their wings and making small cooing sounds. Some sat on nests, then exchanged places with their mates. All of the movement, as 10,000 birds pecked in their feed boxes and flew in short bursts around the lofts, created a whirling, swirling mass of activity.

Marilyn stood silently for a long time as she watched the pigeons. Finally in her naive manner of speaking, she turned to Paul and said, "I have never seen so many wings in my whole life." Most people might have commented on the number of birds, but Marilyn saw wings, fluttering, flapping and folding smoothly against plump feathered bodies. Perhaps wings symbolized something important to Marilyn, a freedom she didn't have, an ability to fly away at will.

The pigeons must have interested Marilyn more than the other stock raised on the ranch since she showed no interest in the hogs and beef cattle that also brought in revenue to sustain the property. Somehow, fluttery birds fit the image of Marilyn Monroe better then stocky cattle or fat pigs.

Many years later Paul remembered the remark in the pigeon lofts because it was so typical of Marilyn's manner of speaking, and because it was one of the few conversations he had with her. Thinking back on Marilyn's visit, Paul said, "Unlike most of our guests, I never got to know her because she kept to herself. Most of her meals, she requested delivered to the guest house where she stayed. She had come for the solitude of the desert and seemed content to remain alone without interacting with other visitors."

Marilyn, nicknamed "The Blonde Bombshell," was at the height of her career when she came to hide out at Singing Tree Ranch. She had acted in a number of movies beginning in 1947 with a bit part in *The Shocking Miss Pilgrim*, followed by *Dangerous Years* (1947) and **Scudda Hoo! Scudda Hay!** (1948). At this point, 20th Century-Fox decided not to renew her contract. With the $150 a week she had been receiving cut off, she went back to modeling and acting school.

Life for Norma Jean Mortensen, her birth name, had never been easy. Her father abandoned her mother before Marilyn was born in Los Angeles General Hospital. She grew up never knowing for sure who her father was. Her mother, Gladys, worked as a film cutter at RKO Studios and had her own problems. Continuously fighting mental illness, in and out of mental institutions, she left her daughter to the foster home system.

In one home when she was two years old, Norma Jean (Marilyn) was nearly smothered to death. In another at age six, she barely escaped being raped. At nine she worked in the kitchen of Los Angeles Orphans Home for five cents a month. It was quite a system, since one penny was taken back every Sunday for church. By age sixteen, Norma Jean had a job in an aircraft plant and in an effort to escape her orphanage life, married a man, she called Daddy. When he went into the military, she turned to modeling to support herself. They divorced four years later.

It was Howard Hughes, head of RKO Studios, who saw pictures of Norma Jean and ordered a screen test, but an agent decided 20th Century Fox would be a better choice because it was a larger, more prestigious studio. Her name was changed from Norma Jean Mortensen to Norma Jean Baker to Marilyn Monroe, although, she preferred Jean Monroe. Her mother's maiden name was Monroe and there was some indication she may have been a descendant of President James Monroe, although it was never definitely established.

After her first small parts in three films for Fox in 1947-48, Columbia Pictures signed her up for *Ladies of the Chorus* (1948) where she sang two numbers. The critics liked her, but didn't like the movie and Columbia dropped her. Once again she returned to modeling.

It was in 1949 that Marilyn posed nude for the now famous calendar shot which appeared some years later in a 1953 *Playboy Magazine* as their first centerfold. The next year, 1950, she appeared in five films. It was in *The Asphalt Jungle* and *All About Eve* that she acquired her sexy blond image.

Through the early 1950's she appeared in *Love Nest* (1951) *Monkey Business* (1952) and *Gentlemen Prefer Blonds* (1953). She also met Joe DiMaggio, the famous New York Yankees slugger. The public liked Marilyn Monroe and she was given a part along with Betty Grable, Lauren Bacall and Rory Calhoun in *How to Marry a Millionaire* (1953). Her sexy image was solidly established and she married Joe DiMaggio. *The Seven Year Itch* (1955) not only showed her talent for comedy, but showcased the iconic image of her, standing above a subway grate with her white dress billowing around her waist.

By 1955, Marilyn was divorced from her eight-month marriage to Joe DiMaggio and her work habits began to deteriorate. She was continually late to the sets, tended to be uncooperative, and seemed to have trouble learning her lines. She did have success, however, with *Bus Stop* (1956) and *Some Like It Hot* (1959) with Tony Curtis and Jack Lemon. She also married playwright, Arthur Miller, which may seem an unlikely liaison, but most of the real Marilyn was never revealed to the public.

Who knew, for example, that ten years earlier at age sixteen while working in the aircraft plant, she owned over 200 books. Among them were the authors Tolstoy, Walt Whitman, and Milton. Her favorite records were works by Beethoven and during her acting years, she could often be seen carrying around *The Biography of Abraham Lincoln.*

Marilyn appeared in *Let's Make Love* (1960) with Tony Randall and Yves Montand. Her final film, *The Misfits* (1961) with Clark Gable was the last movie for both Gable and Monroe. He passed away that year from a heart attack. Marilyn died in 1962 at age 36.

The Los Angeles coroner ruled it a probable suicide from an overdose of sleeping pills, but questions remain concerning her death. John W. Miner, an L.A. County Prosecutor who was present at her autopsy, was never convinced she killed herself. He stated it was the most bizarre case in American history because after the autopsy, every body specimen which could have proved she did not kill herself, disappeared overnight.

The toxic level of barbiturates found, indicated she would have had to take 60 to 70 pills, yet her stomach was almost completely empty. Miner is also the only person who was privy to tapes made by her psychiatrist that outlined her future plans, desire to be taken seriously and her comments about President John F. Kennedy and Robert F. Kennedy, U.S. Attorney General at the time. Only because the psychiatrist was considered a possible suspect in Marilyn's death, did he reveal their confidental contents to Miner, the investigating officer. Miner maintained that anyone who heard the tapes would conclude there was no possible way this woman could have killed herself. The tapes were likely destroyed upon the death of the psychiatrist and Miner passed away in 2011 still believing Marilyn was most likely murdered.

Marilyn made only thirty films in her short lifetime, but she is remembered for her sexy blond image by those who saw her movies and those who simply know of her as the shapely platinum blond in the billowing white dress standing on the subway grate.

What the public doesn't know about her are some of the things which made her the individual she was: an outstanding teenage softball player and a suggested wife for Prince Rainer of Monaco before he married Grace Kelly. Marilyn never graduated from high school, she wore glasses, was one of the first Los Angeles natives to become a movie star, possessed an IQ of 168, higher than John F. Kennedy's 129. Few people know that Elton John's song, *"Candle in the Wind,"* was originally written about Marilyn and then changed to fit Princess Diana after her death.

Marilyn could never have anticipated the famous form-fitting white dress she wore while standing above the subway grate, would be purchased by another movie star, Debbie Reynolds, that the black dress sewn onto her body for the film *Some Like It Hot* would be valued at $200,000, and her JFK birthday gown would bring $1,000,000 at auction. She never made more than $100,000 per picture even though other female stars were earning much more.

Marilyn's too-short life may best be summed up by a few of her quotes.

(About her famous nude calendar pose) *"My sin has been no more than I have written, posing for the nude because I desperately need 50 dollars to get my car out of hock."*

"People had a habit of looking at me as if I were some kind of mirror instead of a person. They didn't see me, they saw their own lewd thoughts..."

"The truth is I've never fooled anyone. I've let people fool themselves. They didn't bother to find out who and what I was. Instead they would invent a character for me."

"Sometimes I think it would be easier to avoid old age, to die young, but then you'd never complete your life would you? You'd never wholly know yourself."

Since Marilyn did die young at age 36, there has always been speculation on whether it was an accident, suicide or murder. It will probably always be a question, but from the known evidence provided by the Los Angeles coroner, Thomas Noguchi who performed the autopsy, the level of Nembutal in her bloodstream was 4.5 milligrams per 100, which would be 40 to 50 capsules, an amount difficult to take by accident.

As for Marilyn's week of privacy in the desert at Janet Gaynor and Paul Gregory's Singing Tree Ranch, it may have been an attempt by Marilyn to heal herself. Her own words tell us more about her than any kind of observation. She once said, *"I restore myself when I'm alone. A career is born in public-- talent in private."*

If Marilyn had turned to the solitude of the desert more often and spent more time at Singing Tree Ranch in the guest house by herself, or with Janet and Paul, sincere people unconcerned with image and public perception, one could speculate that her life might have been radically different.

UNKNOWN IN HIS OWN COUNTRY
Robert McAlmon

Hardly a household name, Robert McAlmon is nevertheless recognized in the revered cannon of American authors even though he is virtually unknown by most Americans. He was a close friend of Gore Vidal's father, and an integral member of the revered early Twentieth Century European writing community. Ezra Pound and F. Scott Fitzgerald insisted McAlmon was a better writer than Hemingway, that his work was tougher and more courageous. In spite of his reputation as a central figure in the "lost generation" of expatriate writers in Paris during the 1920's, he remains undiscovered by Americans.

McAlmon was born in Clifton, Kansas in 1896. The son of an itinerant Presbyterian minister and youngest of ten children, he grew up in the simple, rural life of the American Midwest, almost opposite that which he experienced in Paris as an adult. His small town upbringing in various settlements throughout South Dakota had a major effect upon some of his best writing and it is quite possible the contrast between the two worlds of his youth and his European experience enhanced his view of humanity and contributed to his writing credibility.

McAlmon's first poems were inspired by the airmen in San Diego where he was stationed after enlisting in the United States Air Corps in 1918. He was 22 and had been attending the University of Minnesota for a semester before he decided to enlist. His choice of military service may have been influenced by his childhood friend, Eugene Vidal. Eugene was an aviator and political figure who taught his son, Gore Vidal, to fly at the age of ten.

One of McAlmon's best received books was *Village: As It Happened Through a Fifteen Year Period* (1924). The setting is a bleak American town and is probably modeled after the years he spent growing up in Madison, South Dakota with his best friend Eugene, Gore Vidal's father. Gore documents the friendship in his own 1990's memoir, *Palimpsest,* which chronicles the scandals and gossip of the most famous people during his time. In *Palimpsest,* Vidal is sometimes shocking with his statements that sex is an urge, love is an impossibility and you should never have sex with someone you might actually like.

After the end of World War I, McAlmon enrolled in the University of Southern California, but only attended a few classes before moving to Chicago and then to New York City in search of freedom and companionship.

In New York after working as a nude male model, he collaborated with William Carlos Williams to form a new magazine entitled *Contact.* They also formed a publishing company, which published McAlmon's own works as well as notables of the time, including Ezra Pound, Marianne Moore, Kay Boyle and Hilda Doolittle.

McAlmon stayed only a year in New York before marrying an English author, Annie Winifred Ellerman who wrote under the pen name of Bryher. She was the daughter of shipping magnate, Sir John Ellerman and she chose the name of an island off the coast of Cornwall, England as her *nom de plume*. According to McAlmon, the marriage was one of convenience, legal only, unromantic and strictly an agreement. It allowed Bryher, whose lover was Hilda Doolittle, to take control of her vast inheritance and it gave McAlmon financial independence. He stayed in London only for a brief time and then left for Paris, which began the most prolific period of his literary career.

McAlmon's **Contact Press** put out works by a group of then unpublishable authors: Gertrude Stein, Ernest Hemingway, Bryher, Ezra Pound, Hilda Doolittle, Marsden Hartley, and William Carlos Williams as well as McAlmon's own works varying from an autobiographical novel to short stories, poetry collections and memoirs from 1923 through 1938. McAlmon's poetry found a wider range of publishers, but his only book with substantial circulation was his memoir of the twenties: **Being Geniuses Together** (1938). He was at the time a drinking buddy with James Joyce and Ernest Hemingway. He took Joyce to his first bullfight and teased Hemingway for his intimate friendship with F. Scott Fitzgerald.

After 1935, McAlmon wrote little and found himself unable to leave France due to the German occupation. To add to his difficulties, he contracted tuberculosis. After escaping to Spain he managed to return to the U.S. in 1940 and join his brother in El Paso, Texas a year later. By 1951, he had moved to a small Southern California desert town in the Coachella Valley. His return to the United States did little to increase his recognition in the land of his birth and his death at age 59 in 1956 in Desert Hot Springs, California was little noted, his brilliant writing career unrecognized.

In contrast to the Paris cosmopolitan environment McAlmon was accustomed to, in the late 1940's and early '50's, Desert Hot Springs was as different as one could get. The town was in the process of transforming from ruralhood to tourist destination with hot water spas, and a year around population. Les Morgan's grocery store was near the corner of West and Pierson, the only school, an elementary, opened in 1946, Public Utility Water Company Inc. formed in 1948, and incorporation of the city was first discussed in 1950. Cabot Yerxa was building his pueblo, a malt shop and a movie house opened, popcorn with butter cost 10 cents. L.W. Coffee was drawing celebrities to his hot water mineral baths. For use of the heated pools, a ticket cost 83 cents plus 17 cents tax for the day. A post office was built and the first bank was not far off. A new two-bedroom house could be purchased for $5,000. Things were definitely happening in Desert Hot Springs, but it was still a small town in the process of establishing its unique identity based upon health from naturally heated mineral water.

After McAlmon's success in France and his affiliation with noted writers, poets and literary giants of the time, when he returned to the U.S. and ultimately settled in Desert Hot Springs, he was not just virtually unknown, but must have suffered from culture shock. Perhaps after the damp days along the Seine in Paris and his affliction with tuberculosis, he may have welcomed the dry, sunny desert as a place of recovery. The healthful climate and rejuvenating hot water attracted many of the city's residents and visitors.

In a typewritten letter McAlmon sent to his friend, Bob Wetterau, on Oct. 8, 1951, he wrote.... *It is very nice here, with one very fine restaurant when I want to eat out, and still quiet. My sister bought a house and I am living in it. She and other sisters will drive down now and then to see me, and I hope they don't bring elderly women friends as one did last weekend. But she did cook, fill the ref iferator (sic) with her own canned fruits and fresh fruits, vegs. (sic) etc. Can't kick much."*

He went on to say he got his mail at the post office and his house at 66-299 2nd Street was eight blocks from the town market. In addition he wrote that A.A. Borrows real estate agent next to the post office could give instructions on how to get to his place should his friend be passing through and want to see him. He thanked Bob Wetterau for dinner and for meeting Wetterau's "likeable wife."

McAlmon also wrote: "*I had more of a hangover the next day than I've had for a long time, as I hadn't and am not drinking much,..*" One might conclude that during these last years of his life, he had given up the high life and was living modestly with help from his sisters in a house he did not own.

While seemingly isolated from other literary figures, he did become friends with other notables, one of whom was the actor and philanthropist, Paul Newman. The rest of his life and friends during this period back in the country of his birth is unrecorded and unknown.

McAlmon would never know of his biography, **McAlmon and the Lost Generation,** published in 1962 twelve years after his death or that a number of his books were reissued. **There Was a Rustle of Silk Stockings** (1963) **Being Geniuses Together** (1968) **Miss Knight and Others** (1992). No doubt he would have been happy to see **Village, Post-Adolescence** and **Miss Knight and Others** in their first American editions – all put out by the University of New Mexico Press in the 1990's.

But his last years, living quietly in Desert Hot Springs reveal very little about this author and poet. With his entire writing and publishing career having taken place in Europe, the American public remains largely unaware of the brilliant man from Kansas who made his mark upon the literary world from across the ocean. As one of those celebrities who chose to live out his final days in the desert, he may have recovered some of his health, but he never recovered the literary status he'd achieved in Paris. During the last years of his life, his neighbors in Desert Hot Springs had no idea of his accomplishments and thought of him only as the gentleman who lived by himself on 2nd street.

Palimpsest – *a parchment or tablet which has been reused after previous writing has been erased.*

DUNE BUGGY MAN
Chuck Connors

Driving the dune buggy over a bumpy gravel road to the top of the hill and parking it close to the door felt good, as it always did. The children would be excited and already waiting inside for his arrival. He gave a soft tap to the horn as a signal he was there and ready to go.

Chuck Connors had arrived at Angel View Crippled Children's Hospital to give dune buggy rides to the youngsters who were mobile enough to hang on and enjoy the thrill of the open vehicle, bouncing along desert trails and sliding up and over sand dunes.

Connors was a father with children of his own, which gave him a special bond with those youngsters afflicted with physical problems. If he could provide a little fun for the less fortunate, he was anxious to do so. In the 1960's when Connors was visiting Desert Hot Springs, giving dune buggy rides to the disabled residents of Angel View was something he could do and it gave him great pleasure.

At 6'5" and a trim 215 pounds, Connors was a powerful man who had used his exceptional physique to excel at sports. Athletics had always been his love and driving force. While still in his teens, twenty-seven college sports scholarships were offered to him, but it was Seton Hall he chose. His time there was cut short when he left to enlist in the army and became a tank-warfare instructor in Kentucky, after which he was promoted to a position at the West Point Military Academy.

In 1946 with the war over, he could focus once again on athletics. His army experience, no doubt, helped condition him for his sports career. He took a job playing professional basketball for the Boston Celtics, but since his first love was baseball, he then moved to spring training with the Brooklyn Dodgers. By 1951 he had signed with the Chicago Cubs and later moved to the Los Angeles Angels. It was at an Angels game that an unusual event took his life on a new turn.

A baseball fan who was a casting director for MGM spotted Connors at the ball game in Los Angeles. Impressed with his imposing presence, the director approached him for a movie role as a prize-fighter. Even though the part ultimately went to Aldo Ray, it launched Kevin Joseph Aloysius Connors on a movie and TV career. Chuck, the name he used for his entire professional life came from his own words, words he used when playing first base at Seton Hall; "*Chuck it to me, baby – Chuck it to me.*"

No doubt his superb physique helped him obtain more movie roles in the next several years. But entering into his new career with gusto and using every opportunity to learn and refine his ability to act, may have been even more important in launching him into the world of movies. After playing parts in twenty films, ironically, it was a television series, The Rifleman, that catapulted his name to a household word.

It was during the time his fame was multiplying as he played Lucas McCain, one of TV's first single parents, on 168 episodes of **The Rifleman** (1958-1963), that the Santucci family recognized him as the star he was when he came to their Capri Restaurant in Desert Hot Springs in the 1960's. By then his career in movies included, **Pat and Mike** with Spencer Tracy and Katharine Hepburn (1952), **South Sea Woman** opposite Burt Lancaster (1953), **Old Yeller** (1957) and **Soylent Green** (1973) with Charlton Heston. In later years he played a slave owner in the 1977 miniseries, **Roots** and stared in the 1985 ABC TV series, **Spencer for Hire.**

Julia Santucci remembers him as an extremely nice person. They often had long discussions during dinner. Connors talked about his four sons and how they should grow up. In his biography, he is quoted as saying. "*I don't want my kids growing up believing that there is nothing destructive in the world. I want them to know that there is good and bad in the world, that you can be hurt physically, that guns can kill you, that drugs are bad for you, that not everyone means well.*"

While in the desert, he also demonstrated his concern for children in general with his visits to Angel View Crippled Children's Home. Most times he was in Desert Hot Springs, he'd find time to drive his dune buggy to Angel View and spend the afternoon taking crippled children for rides out amongst the creosote and saltbush.

For many of the physically disabled children, these outings were the most exciting thing they could think of. Whether they saw Connors on TV or not, the big man with the big smile made their day with a wild trip they never forgot. They wouldn't have cared that he was elected to the Cowboy Hall of fame (which came much later in 1991) or that he was inducted into the Hall of Great Western Performers of the National Cowboy and Western Heritage Museum or that he played baseball for the Dodgers. All that mattered to them was piling into the dune buggy and hanging on for the ride of their lives.

His service to the children of Angel View was one of the reasons, the Santuccis valued Chuck's friendship and felt privileged to serve him at their restaurant. Kevin Joseph Aloysius "Chuck" Connors was one of those special people who enriched the lives of those around him. John Santucci said, "Not every celebrity is someone one would want to know personally."

Adults as well as children were drawn to this masterful television cowboy. In 1973 at Richard Nixon's Western White House in San Clemente, Chuck Connors was introduced to

Secretary General Leonid Brezhnev of the Soviet Union. They hit it off immediately, probably due somewhat to the fact that *The Rifleman* was one of the few American shows allowed on Soviet TV. Connors traveled to the Soviet Union twice, in 1973 and 1982 as a friend of Brezhnev and at one point in their relationship, Connors presented Brezhnev with two colt guns. Yet, when Brezhnev died, Connors was not allowed to be a part of the official American delegation.

During the era of Chuck Connors' stardom, smoking was not only an accepted habit, but was also considered suave and sophisticated. Connors was an avid smoker which, no doubt, contributed to his death from lung cancer in 1992 at age seventy-one.

His biography states that "*although Chuck Connors is gone, he still lives on as "The Rifleman.*" For the Santucci family, "Chuck it to me" Connors stays in their memories because of his loving dedication to children. Over fifty years have passed since they first grew to know the big athletic man who went out of his way to bring some excitement into the lives of crippled children. Others may remember him as "The Riffleman," but for the Santucci family and some very special people from Angel View, "Dune Buggy Man" embodies the real spirit of Chuck Connors.

"King of Hollywood"
Clark Gable

When Clark Gable and his sixth wife, Kay Spreckles, appeared at the groundbreaking ceremony for a new wing at Angel View Crippled Children's Foundation in Desert Hot Springs, no one would have guessed Gable would die within the year. Speculation had it that his crash diet to reduce from 230 pounds to 190 for his role in *The Misfits,* his last film, may have triggered his heart attack. There was talk that physical exertion demanded by the movie he was filming with Marilyn Monroe triggered the attack. But his wife, Kay, said it was the tension that killed him, "the eternal waiting, waiting, waiting," on the set. He was fifty-nine.

Raye Horton of Desert Hot Springs was one of those who had the experience of meeting Gable that day at Angel View. Nearly fifty years later, she still recalls Gable as the dashing Rhett Butler in **Gone With the Wind** and how she felt meeting "The King of Hollywood."

Raye was no starstruck dreamer. She simply represented the way Clark Gable in his movie roles affected his audience. Raye was a down-to-earth person and a hard worker. She met Alan Horton a year after he opened his grocery store in Desert Hot Springs in 1946. Their romance blossomed quickly and within a few months they repeated wedding vows that would bind them together for the rest of their lives.

Running a business in a remote desert community at that time was not as simple as it might seem. Since there was no bank in town, the Hortons had to make a trip to Palm Springs every day to deposit their receipts and get change for the cash register. After taking care of their banking needs, they also picked up mail for residents living north of Palm Springs and delivered it to Betty Hudspeth, the post mistress of the small Desert Hot Springs post office. Through the grocery store and mail delivery, the Hortons got to know almost everyone in town and as a consequence became major players in the lives of people living in the Desert Hot Springs area.

Raye's husband, Alan, helped out at the Boys and Girls Club, joined civic organizations and was especially helpful to Angel View Crippled Children's Foundation, which is how that sunny day in May of 1960, he and Raye ended up standing with a large group of people on a weed-grown lot at the top of Miracle Hill.

Raye distinctly remembers the stinging sand as it swirled around in a storm of pellets and dust picked up from the ground by the helicopter's spinning blades...

* * *

She shielded her face with one hand in front of her eyes and with the other, she tried to hold down the hem of her blue and white-striped dress billowing above her knees. As the helicopter descended and dropped gracefully onto two white strips of cloth pinned to the ground in the shape of an X, the roar of the engine and thump, thump of the blades slowly diminished. Finally, when all was quiet, the turbulent air began to clear. Like a ship from outer space, the copter's door opened and Raye stood transfixed, along with a crowd of dignitaries gathered for the occasion, as Clark Gable and his wife, Kay Aldrich Spreckels, stepped out onto the desert sand.

There he was, Rhett Butler and the "King of Hollywood," wrapped up in the handsome man in navy blue jacket and gray pants striding casually towards the gathered crowd. Raye took a deep breath and focused on his highly polished black loafers. She didn't want to be caught staring at him.

The rest of the ceremony blurred its way to the end with speeches, clapping and handshaking. Raye couldn't have told you how much time had gone by because for her it stood still.

Photographs were taken with Gable, his wife Kay, Ester Eaton and Rose Bertram, who, through her connection with the City of Hope was instrumental in arranging the Gables' appearance. After another round of handshaking and congratulatory comments, Gable and his wife climbed back into the helicopter. With a final wave from one of the biggest movie stars ever, the pilot revved the engine, sent its blades whirling and amid a new cloud of gritty residue and dust, the helicopter rose upwards until all that could be seen was a small dark smudge in the distant sky. The groundbreaking ceremony for Angel View's new 16-bed addition was completed.

Raye, still caught in the magic of Gable's dramatic appearance, stood motionless and speechless, barely able to breathe. Visions of the concluding scene from Gone With the Wind filled her mind - the handsome, dashing Rhett Butler looking up the stairs at the beautiful, pleading Scarlett O'Hara and saying, "Frankly, My Dear, I don't give a damn."

Raye didn't know whether her head pounded from the excitement of shaking the hand of Clark Gable or from the throbbing sound of the helicopter, echoing from nearby foothills. Alan was urging her to the car so he could get back to the store, but Raye was in no hurry. She was still in Atlanta at Tara with the handsome Rhett Butler.

* * *

The helicopter that delivered Clark Gable to the Angel View ground breaking also had on board movie star and Olympic ice skater, Sonja Henie, as well as Ray Ryan, owner of the Mirador Hotel in Palm Springs and top dog of the social scene. Raye doesn't remember them, nor had she paid much attention to the ceremony. While the Indian dancers performed and the Sherman

Institute Band played, her eyes were on Clark Gable. Dr. Robert Bingham, clinic medical director, gave a long report on the activities at Angel View and Palm Springs mayor, Frank Bogert, greeted the crowd. After which Aubrey Wardman, benefactor, turned the first chunk of sod with a gold-painted shovel. Raye doesn't even recall these activities.

It's not surprising that Raye felt starstruck at the sight of Clark Gable. Her reaction echoed that of millions of women and accounts for Gable's nickname, "The King of Hollywood." In time Gable grew tired of his nickname and stated, "This 'King' stuff is pure bullshit...I'm just a lucky slob from Ohio. I happened to be in the right place at the right time." Robert Taylor disagreed and summed up Gable with these words, (Gable) "was a great, great guy and certainly one of the great stars of all times, if not the greatest. I think that I sincerely doubt that there will ever be another like Clark Gable, he was one of a kind."

Gable's performance in the 1939 Civil War Epic, *Gone With the Wind,* earned him his third Academy Award for best actor. It was Gable's first film in Technicolor and was so popular it was re-released seven times, the most recent in 1998. Gable once said that whenever his career began to fade, it was brought back to life with a re-release of *Gone With the Wind.*

Originally Gary Cooper had been chosen to play the role of Rhett Butler, but he turned it down. He is quoted as saying, "*Gone With the Wind* is going to be the biggest flop in Hollywood history. I'm glad it'll be Clark Gable who's falling flat on his nose, not me." Even Gable was not enthusiastic about the role in the beginning. Carole Lombard had wanted to play his leading lady, Scarlet, and bought him the bestselling book. He refused to read it.

With all of Gable's masculine appeal on and off the silver screen, few would guess that his costar, Vivien Leigh, in *Gone With the Wind*, complained during the filming about Gable's bad breath which was attributed to his false teeth. But he was also a heavy drinker and smoker. He regularly went through three packs of unfiltered cigarettes a day, several cigars and filled his pipe with tobacco at least twice. Fortunately his adoring fans in their theater seats would never be aware of this aspect of their idol.

As Hollywood's most important leading man in the 1930's Gable had an effect on men as well as women. In the movie, *It Happened One Night,* (1934) where he played opposite Claudette Colbert, he took off his shirt and revealed he was not wearing an undershirt. Sales of undershirts around the country declined over the next few months.

Gable's road to popularity was not without detours and breakdowns. In the beginning he failed numerous screen tests and played a number of supporting roles before his popularity rocketed. Darryl Zanuck of Warner Bros. said, "His ears are too big and he looks like an ape." But ultimately his charisma won out and he was paired with some of the top female stars of the era, Jean Harlow, Joan Crawford, Norma Shearer, Greta Garbo, Myrna Loy, Lana Turner and Marilyn Monroe in his last movie, *The Misfits,* just before his death. It was also Marilyn's last movie. In all, Gable was in seventy-two movies, during a career beginning in 1924 and lasting until 1961.

His personal life was less successful than his movie career. He had six wives and numerous liaisons between and during his marriages. His only child during his lifetime was born out of wedlock to Loretta Young, who refused to acknowledge the girl was his, but did, however, give permission to reveal the truth after her own death. Kay Spreckles bore his second child, a boy, four months after Gable's death.

Of his six wives, Carole Lombard, was the one with whom he found real happiness. He expressed it with these words, "You can trust that little screwball with your life or your hopes or your weaknesses, and she wouldn't even know how to think about letting you down." Tragedy struck when the twin-engine DC-3 carrying Lombard on a tour to sell war bonds in 1942 crashed near Las Vegas killing all aboard. As the first war-related female death of World War II, President Franklin D. Roosevelt sent Gable a personal letter of condolence.

Gable achieved the rank of captain in World War II and flew combat missions, mostly in the United Kingdom at RAF Polebrook. He was awarded the Air Medal and Distinguished Flying Cross.

Raye Horton feels lucky to have had the experience of meeting Clark Gable on that day in May at Angel View. She never could have dreamed at the time that he had only a few short months to live. Nearly fifty years later, she still recalls the dashing Rhett Butler and feels privileged to have met "The King of Hollywood."

Nature Boy
Eden Ahbez

"There was a boy, a very sad and lonely boy." These words from **"Nature Boy,"** a popular 1950's song, probably describe the life of its composer, Eden Ahbez, as well as any words could. While few may recall his name, one of his hauntingly beautiful songs lives on long after its introduction by Nat King Cole in 1948 when every radio disc jockey played it multiple times a day.

John Furbee, a retired pharmacist and owner of the only drug store in Desert Hot Springs during the 1970's, remembers Ahbez as a local character. "He looked like a typical desert rat," Furbee said, "a small man, flowing gray hair and long white beard. He usually wore coveralls and a long-sleeved shirt, clean, but wrinkled. Sometimes he had on leather sandals that looked like they were falling apart. Once or twice I saw he wore heavy work boots."

From the time Furbee purchased his pharmacy in 1969, Ahbez was a regular, showing up almost daily to use the pay phone inside the store. "I never talked with him that much," Furbee said, "but Lola knew him well. Lola Skuse ran the store, knew everyone and everything going on in and out of town. Lola liked Ahbez. She gave me one of his cassettes with a bunch of his songs on it. **'Nature Boy'** was the lead song, but he also had one entitled **'Nature Girl.'** I guess the only song to make the big time was **'Nature Boy'** and that was due to Nat King Cole's recording of it. Dinah Shore and Frank Sinatra made recordings of it, too, so that helped make it a number one hit. I took a liking to Eden's music and used to listen to it when I didn't have my favorite classical music playing."

Eden, who always insisted his name be spelled only with lower case letters, wrote the words and music while camping in Tahquitz Canyon in the Coachella Valley. Frank Bogert, mayor of Palm Springs during its heyday as a movie star playground, always thought Eden's inspiration came from his association with Peter William (Bill) Pester, the well-remembered hermit of Palm Springs. Pester certainly fit the "nature boy" description as well as Ahbez.

While Ahbez lived for a part of his life in Big Tujunga Canyon near Los Angeles, he visited Pester at his small rustic cabin in Palm Canyon and most likely the hot spring area in nearby Chino Canyon where Pester spent the summers. Pester survived by carving walking sticks from the tough, blossom stalk of native palm trees and peddling them to tourists. Flint knapping arrowheads and selling postcards added to his meager income. On weekends in downtown Palm Springs he'd set up a telescope and charge 10 cents to view Lincoln's profile on a mountain ridge above the city.

No doubt Ahbez was drawn to Pester because of their similar primitive life styles, but whether the song, **"Nature Boy,"** came from Ahbez's personal experiences or from his visits with Pester, is hard to say. Another possibility for the name may be his relationship with a raw food cafe in Hollywood that followed a philosophy of returning to nature. They called their followers, "Nature Boys."

One of his songs, **"Anna Was Mine,"** definitely related to his wife, Anna. **"Nature Girl"** probably was for his daughter, Zuma. Other songs on a CD and tape put out by Golden World Enterprises of Desert Hot Springs in 1995 are: **"The Secret of Love," "As the Wind," "Jerusalem," "Divine Melody," "The Path,"** and **"No Bums Allowed."**

Born in 1908 in Brooklyn, N.Y. Ahbez was one of thirteen orphaned children who were placed in foster homes. He was sent to the old Brooklyn Hebrew Orphan Asylum, then adopted and raised in Kansas, where he played piano and worked as a dance band leader. After moving to Los Angeles in 1941, he became enamored with natural living and health food to the extent they became his primary focus. To learn how other people lived with nature and found access to health food, Ahbez set out on a trek across the United States. He traveled only on foot and sought the company of those living the kind of life he wanted for himself. After completing his walk across the country, he was so inspired, he made the journey once again. He also rode the rails and crossed the U.S. at least eight times.

Back in California, his wanderings included time spent in Big Tujunga Canyon in Los Angeles where he found a kindred soul, Anna Jacobsen. He married her and fathered a daughter, Zuma, who could have been called "nature girl" since her parents seldom put any clothes on her as she ran about their remote canyon camp.

Some of their time was spent in Santa Barbara, and Palm Springs, but after his wife died, Ahbez began looking for a place to settle where he could continue to live the natural way he'd focused on and felt so passionate about. The sparsely settled area north of Palm Springs around the tiny community of Desert Hot Springs suited him and became his choice for the rest of his life.

It was there at his drug store that John Furbee became familiar with Ahbez. Furbee recalls Ahbez used flute music in his songs. "He carved his own flutes from bamboo. He gave one to my delivery boy. I never heard him try to play it so I don't know how good it sounded," Furbee recalls. "There was a big spread about him in *Life Magazine* and I remember reading something he said about his music, '*The words were hard, the music was easy*.' I always wondered about that and thought maybe his living alone so much made it harder for him to come up with the right words."

Furbee reminisced about his first drug store located on Palm Drive in a two story building with apartments on the second floor. "Robert Altman filmed a movie in Desert Hot Springs the year I remodeled the first floor and the film crew and actors rented the second floor apartments. I thought the rooms were really awful, old furniture, sagging beds, but they seemed to like them, so that's where they stayed and filmed.

"The drugstore needed some modernizing, too, so I brought it up to date. The phone company took out the public pay phone during the remodeling and wouldn't put it back. A new pay phone was installed outside just up the block near the corner of Pierson and Palm. So that's where everybody went to make their calls. I liked Ahbez, he never made a fuss, and I missed seeing him after the phone was moved out of the drugstore. The only times I saw Ahbez after that were when he needed something from the pharmacy and I never knew exactly where he lived. I think he was happy out of the public eye and hidden away in a remote spot of his choosing.

"He died in 1995, I think it was. He was 86 or 87 by then, so I guess the nature boy lifestyle must have agreed with him. I have no idea if he was still using the pay phone on the corner up to the time of his death, but I guess he could've. It's still there, you know. It's been forty years now that phone has been out there on the side of the building and people still use it. But with everybody having cell phones these days, I wonder how much longer it will last. I think we should name it the Nature Boy Phone. He'd like that, I think. It'd be a way for people to remember him."

The pay phone mounted on the wall at the corner of Palm and Pierson was removed in 2010 when the entire block of buildings was renovated.

T-Shirts and Jeans
John Travolta

Ellen Ridley was a sister of John Travolta. She lived at Desert Willow Ranch in the rural area just east of Desert Hot Springs. The ranch had originally been purchased in 1918 for 10 cents an acre. In the 1920's and 30's it changed hands several times. An entrepreneur named Matt MacDonald purchased it for 25 cents an acre and sold it for the enormous profit of 50 cents an acre. Jimmy Ridley who was never seen without a cowboy hat, along with his wife, Ellen, were the owners in the 1970's when John Travolta made his frequent visits. It was a great place for him to get away from Hollywood where he was busy pursuing a career in acting.

It was during this time that Travolta was often seen on the streets of Desert Hot Springs in his typical casual attire of jeans, boots and T-shirt. It was also during this time that he is affectionately remembered for putting on a fund raising show for the local grade school. Using his contacts in the acting and music world of Hollywood, he gathered together a crew of his buddies who were also movie hopefuls, to put on a live stage performance at the Desert Hot Springs local movie theater. Not only was it great fun for the townspeople, it raised money to help the school. Almost everyone living in Desert Hot Springs during that time remembers the show and many also recall Travolta's efforts to help the Boys and Girls Club.

Of the six children born to the Englewood, New Jersey family of Helen and Salvatore Travolta, John was the youngest.

His mother was involved with singing and acting and all of her children followed in her footsteps. Of the six siblings, only John and Ellen left the east coast to settle in California. John was counting on Hollywood rather than New York as a more likely place for him to succeed and it appears he made an excellent choice. Ellen also gained success on the west coast with parts in TV shows. She appeared in *General Hospital, Charles In Charge,* and several times as the mother of one of his students after Travolta got the lead in *Welcome Back Kotter.*

Like so many of the movie stars who lived in the Los Angeles area, Travolta viewed the desert as an easy getaway since the drive from the coast could be made in less than two hours. When he came to visit his older sister, Ellen, it was a relaxing change for him. Roaming the 110 acres of Desert Willow Ranch was fine for enjoying the desert, but Travolta often preferred spending his time in town. Locals were used to seeing him, but since he was not yet well-known, they paid little attention.

The Santucci family, operators of the Capri Restaurant and Steak House in Desert Hot Springs, remembers when Travolta got the role of Vinnie Barbarino in *Welcome Back Kotter.* The sitcom consisted of all kinds of high school activities and high jinks, most of it very funny but with a serious undertone. The Santuccis recall how excited Travolta was when he came to the restaurant for dinner after being chosen for the Barbarino character. They had known he was pursuing an acting career and had had numerous minor roles plus the one he played in a stage version of *Grease* in 1972, but they also knew he was not a big star, just another aspiring actor.

They never dreamed at that time that this jeans and T-shirt clad young man would make a name for himself and become as well known as Burt Reynolds, Robert Redford or any of the bigger-than-life movie stars. They could never have guessed he would be credited with inspiring the Disco phenomenon as a result of his part in the movie, *Saturday Night Fever* in 1977, or that in the 1980's, he would be the inspiration for the country music craze that swept the nation due to the influence of **Urban Cowboy**. For John and Julia Santucci and their sons working at the restaurant, Travolta was just a nice kid who came in for a meal when he was in town visiting his sister.

Travolta never talked about his background. He had left school at age sixteen to pursue an acting career and made his debut in an off-Broadway production of **Rain.** Other bit roles followed as he worked in show business. He was still only twenty-one when he landed the role in the ABC sitcom, **Welcome Back Kotter.** The show ran from 1975 to 1979 and catapulted him from obscurity into the mainstream of television actors.

A number of the locals who remember John Travolta before he was a huge star, speak of him with affection. They may have seen him in a restaurant and observed his friendly demeanor, or perhaps they exchanged ideas in the local grocery store. They especially remember the fund raising stage show he organized and they all speak of him kindly.

In the late 1970's after his huge success with **Saturday Night Fever,** which critics labeled a latter-day **Rebel Without a Cause** and for which Travolta received his first Academy Award nomination, it wasn't as easy for John to lead a simple, unassuming life wandering freely around a small desert town. Then, after his appearance in the movie, **Grease**, in 1978 and **Urban Cowboy** with Debra Winger in the early 1980's, his visits to the desert weren't the same. With **Grease** and **Saturday Night Fever** breaking records for the most economically successful films of the decade, Travolta's life changed completely. He had attained the status of a major player in the movie industry and free time for relaxing quietly in the desert was no longer possible.

His career continued with lead roles in a wide variety of movies and his reputation see-sawed, depending upon the box office success or failure of his latest film. Then in 1994, a role in **Pulp Fiction** directed by Quentin Tarantino, brought Travolta true fame and firmly established him as a major movie star. In addition, the film also garnered him his second Academy Award nomination.

As stardom crowned Travolta, he acquired the possessions available only to the super wealthy. His multimillion dollar estate in Florida is located on an airport runway that allows him to taxi right up to his home in his own 707-138 airplane named Jett Clipper Ella in honor of his son, Jett, and daughter, Ella. While it is one of five planes he owns and flies, he uses it for charity purposes as well as personal. After the 2010 earthquake in Haiti, he flew it filled with doctors, supplies and Scientology's volunteer ministers to Haiti. And in June, 2010, on a trip to South Africa, he and his wife donated $10,000 to the Nelson Mandela Children's Fund. Travolta is a certified pilot. One wonders if he ever thinks back to mornings spent in Desert Hot Springs with the local hardware store owner flying remote controlled model airplanes out over the raw desert.

Travolta's life has also had its share of tragedy, beginning with his relationship with actress Diana Hyland who died of breast cancer in 1977. He married another actress, Kelly Preston in 1991 and their first child, Jett, died in The Bahamas from a seizure. Jett was autistic and suffered from seizures throughout his short life of sixteen years. To make matters worse, the couple had to deal with a multimillion dollar extortion plot revolving around the signing of papers concerning their son's death. So extensive was the plot, it even involved former U. S. Senator, Pleasant Bridgewater, who later resigned because of the allegations of abetment and conspiracy to extort charged against her.

While famous people are revered for their professional accomplishments, their private lives are not always admirable. It is quite possible we wouldn't like them as next door neighbors or friends. Others develop reputations showing their personable side before they become stars and the best of them like John Travolta continue to be the same kind of person even after their names are headliners.

Fame and fortune carry with them huge responsibilities and for many people with an altered lifestyle dictated by their wealth and celebrity status, it can be difficult for them to see themselves without a sense of self importance. Travolta has never acquired the reputation of someone who is above it all. For those who "knew him when" and hold only fond memories of the young man who went out of his way to aid the grade school in a small desert town, it may be they are privileged to have experienced one of the stars whose fame and fortune never overpowered the real person.

When Travolta, an aspiring actor, wandered around Desert Hot Springs in his T-shirt and jeans, could he or anyone in the town have imagined the white suit he would later wear in *Saturday Night Fever* would be purchased in 1978 by the film critic, Gene Siskel, for $2,000? Even more amazing is that seventeen years after that in 1995, it would be sold again. This time it brought $145,000 at a Christies charity auction.

MYSTERIOUS ENVELOPES
Frank Sinatra

Few celebrities were better known than Frank Sinatra. Yet most of his fans never had the slightest concept of the real man behind the talent. In spite of his reputation as a generous tipper, they could not have imagined the extent of his generosity and only a few were aware of the times he went out of his way to do nice things for people he didn't even know.

Marilyn Monroe once said of him, "He is a man at the top of his profession and is a fine actor as well. You know, he got an Oscar for *From Here to Eternity* (1953). He has helped more people anonymously than anybody else. And the miserable press smears him with lies about his being involved with the Mafia and gangsters. And Frank just takes it."

Marilyn had it right. Frank helped people and in some cases he went to great extents to keep his generosity a secret. One example of his thoughtful gestures involved people in Desert Hot Springs. There were times he'd give a six-inch high stack of white envelopes with names and addresses to his valet, Dante, and ask him to deliver them to the small, less affluent town on the north side of the freeway. Dante had to borrow a car for the errand because he couldn't use one of Sinatra's, since the license plates, FAS 1, FAS 2, all the way to twenty were so distinctive everyone recognized them.

The envelopes contained cash for people in need whom Sinatra had heard about. Sometimes it was to buy a new bicycle for a kid who'd had his stolen, or it might be a house payment for a needy family, or money for a medical bill. Dante's job was to drive up to Desert Hot Springs and slip the envelopes in mailboxes or under doors, whatever it took to get the money to the right address without anyone seeing him. Sinatra simply wanted to help people in need and he didn't want any publicity for doing it.

Julia Santucci and her husband, John, owners of the Capri Restaurant in Desert Hot Springs, remember Sinatra from the many times he came there for a good steak. For many years the Capri included "Steak Sinatra" as one of their menu choices. Julia recalls Sinatra being asked for a contribution to build a pool for the Desert Hot Springs Boys and Girls Club. She said, "He forked over a big amount, I think it was enough to cover the entire cost. There was talk of naming the pool after him, but he didn't want that."

Other townspeople say Sinatra's contribution was a large amount, but not enough to cover the whole project and more money still had to be raised. If you ask the kids at the Boys and Girls Club today where the money came from to build their pool, they have no idea because Sinatra was able to keep his contribution quiet.

Sinatra had a way of looking after the little guy, but he also gave large amounts for specific projects. According to Judge Jim Walsworth, his personal attorney, Sinatra paid off the $120,000 mortgage of the St. Louis Catholic Church in Cathedral City, as well as the mortgage at Temple Isaiah in Palm Springs.

When Joe Louis, heavyweight boxing champion of the world from 1937-1949, had heart trouble, Sinatra sent him back East to the noted heart specialist, William DeBakey, then brought him back to the Sinatra compound to recover. Later in the 1970s he got Louis a job as casino host at Caesars Palace in Las Vegas. All he had to do was be there and people would come in because they wanted their picture taken with him. Everyone gave Caesars Palace credit for helping Louis, but it was really Sinatra who came up with the idea and arranged it. The public never knew Sinatra was involved. In 1981 when Joe Louis died, his funeral was held in Caesars Palace Sports Pavilion. Frank Sinatra and the Rev. Jesse Jackson delivered the eulogies.

It was in 1976 that Sinatra needed a judge to perform the marriage ceremony for his wedding to Barbara Marx in Rancho Mirage. Judge Walsworth, an Orange County Superior Court judge, was asked to perform the ceremony, but his participation came about in a rather peculiar way.

During the judge's term on the bench, Sinatra had written a letter to him commending him on some of the positions he'd taken. Sinatra had advised him to "keep up the good work." The judge wrote back thanking Sinatra for his interest. These two letters were the extent of their relationship until Sinatra began looking for an official to perform his wedding ceremony. The Coachella Valley judge best known to Sinatra and most logical pick was not available at the time of the wedding. Deciding among the others in the area was problematic due to concerns about alienating the ones not asked. As the decision became potentially more involved with Riverside County politics, Sinatra solved the problem. He said to his right hand man, "Why don't you get that guy over in Orange County?" That guy was Jim Walsworth.

The wedding was to take place in July of 1976 at Sunnylands, the Annenberg Estate, built by Walter and Lenore Annenberg. After the Annenbergs fell in love with the desert as a place for a winter home and getaway, they found an undeveloped site of over 200 acres and began planning their vacation home. Golfing was a major activity for them, so they included a nine hole golf course along with their building plans. The elaborate estate home situated on the edge of the private course, in time became known as the Camp David of the West, due to its hosting of world leaders, summit meetings and high-caliber gatherings. Frank Sinatra couldn't have found a more prestigious setting for marrying the woman with whom he would spend the rest of his life.

As part of the festivities leading up to Sinatra's marriage, Judge Walsworth who had as yet never met Sinatra, was invited to a pre-wedding dinner at Melvyn's Restaurant in Palm Springs. He arrived with his wife and was seated near the window. Sinatra and his family were together at a large table over in a corner and at some time during the early evening, Sinatra asked, "Who is that tall guy in the blue suit?" He was told it was the judge who was going to marry him. Sinatra, thinking the judge comment was a joke, answered, "He's no judge, throw him out." Of course they didn't throw him out. Sinatra simply had never seen him and didn't know what he looked like.

As the story goes, a New York newspaper reporter attending the dinner, heard about the incident and had to be talked out of the headline she wanted to use for the story, **Judge to Marry Sinatra Nearly Expelled from Wedding Dinner.**

Judge Walsworth remembered the day of the big event and said, " It was a virtual Who's Who, with Richard Nixon, Spiro Agnew, Ronald Reagan, Kirk Douglas, Cary Grant, Bette Davis, Gregory Peck, Rosalind Russell, Steve Forbes, and a few guys who looked a little suspect. The best man was Freeman Gosman from the radio show, *Amos and Andy.* The wedding certificate was signed by Ronald Reagan."

Marrying Frank and Barbara led to a more personal connection later when Judge Walsworth became Sinatra's personal attorney. Consequently he knew things about Sinatra the public was never privy to like the white envelopes delivered to Desert Hot Springs.

Judge Walsworth once made the mistake of correcting a reporter, who commented on how nice it was of Caesars Palace to give Joe Louis a token job. "It wasn't Caesars Palace, it was Frank Sinatra who got him that job," Walsworth said.

"Can I quote you?" the reporter asked.

"Absolutely not," answered Walsworth.

A few weeks later a newspaper story appeared with the headline, *Ol Blue Eyes, You can't get away with it.* The story revealed the truth about Sinatra's role in securing the Caesars Palace job for Joe Louis with details even Walsworth didn't know. The reporter had researched and found the information elsewhere. When Walsworth asked Sinatra what he thought of the reporter's story, Sinatra said, "It was O.K. I just wish I knew who the S.O.B. was who told him about it."

"It was the last time I ever mentioned any of his generous deeds while he was alive. He really didn't want anyone to know about this stuff," Walsworth said.

Walsworth also remembered another aspect of Sinatra most people would never suspect. "Sinatra lived on five acres and you couldn't go there without seeing a bunch of dogs and they were never the same ones. He found homes for dogs. If you stayed any amount of time at his compound, you left with a dog. He probably placed fifteen to twenty dogs a month, all of which he'd rescued from the pound."

A lot of people around the country, even though they admired Sinatra for his celebrity status, were also convinced he had connections with the Mafia, but Judge Walsworth, his attorney, agreed with Marilyn Monroe and said, "No, he didn't." Mobsters were certainly seen in the Coachella Valley during the movie star era. It was not unusual to walk into one of the popular restaurants and find several burly men with black suits and cigars hanging out at the bar. People simply accepted their presence and paid no attention. As one woman who grew up during this time put it, "We all knew there were gangsters around and we just ignored it."

It seems sad that Frank Sinatra's public reputation had more to do with the Mob than with his personal generosity. But it was his choice. Ol' Blue Eyes did it his way.

Judge Jim Walsworth's marriage to his second wife took place at Frank Sinatra's home. Sinatra was the best man and Barbara Sinatra was the maid of honor. Afterward a sit-down dinner for 150 people took place. The judge, a resident of the Coachella Valley passed away in 2011.

3 WOMEN
Robert Altman

Movie director and producer, Robert Altman, woke up from a dream in the middle of the night and decided he was going to make a movie revolving around three women. Only half-awake, thoughts of sand dominated his imagery, so he decided the movie had to take place in the desert. He later realized the sand reference came from a gritty residue left on his sheets by his young son who had been playing on the beach before bedtime. Altman's wife was in the hospital, so he was in charge of the child and had let him sleep with him while his mother was away.

In those dark, early morning hours when ideas for the movie, *3 Women,* crystallized in his mind, Altman knew Sissy Spacek would have to be involved. He'd seen her recent performance in *Carrie* and felt certain she had exceptional talent. In the morning he collected his thoughts from the night's unrest and made arrangements to send scouts out to the desert around Palm Springs to look for a filming location. The year was 1977.

Altman already had popular money-making productions to his credit. His 1957 *The James Dean Story*, a documentary meant to capitalize on James Dean's death, was well-received, along with episodes of the TV series, *Bonanza* and *Kraft Mystery Theater.* But experimentation was a constant element in Altman's work, and by the 1970's he had gained a reputation for creating a renaissance in American movie making. Part of it was his penchant for improvisational dialogue as demonstrated in *3 Women.*

As Altman tells it in his own words, "They found this strange place out in Palm Springs where young girls were walking these old people around in this hot water pool. I knew it had to be in the movie."

The strange place with the hot water pool was really Coffee's Bathhouse in Desert Hot Springs, but to Altman, unfamiliar with the area, everything in the desert was Palm Springs. Coffee's was the first natural hot mineral water spa in Desert Hot Springs and when it opened in 1941, over 2,000 people showed up to celebrate the wonders of the hot water. The city's population at the time was under 100. It was L.W. Coffee's vision to create a world class spa that sparked his layout of streets and development of lots for homes in the newly emerging town.

For six years, Coffee's was the place to take the waters for both celebrities and common people, until a tragic fire in 1947 destroyed the wooden building. But the replacement spa was grandiose and over four times the size of the original. It was the largest and most up-to-date, reinforced concrete structure of its kind on the Pacific Coast. Calling it the "Finest Health Spa in America" was probably close to the truth.

In his new facility, Coffee added a therapeutic pool for those who couldn't swim. It was was two feet deep at one end and three feet deep at the other with benches around the sides for sitting. This would have been the pool Altman referred to as "*the strange place with young girls walking these old people around in this hot water pool.*"

When Altman's scouts discovered Coffee's bathhouse in 1977, it had been operating for thirty years and was looking a bit seedy. Altman knew immediately it had the ethereal quality he needed for his film. In **3 Women**, we see Pinky Rose, played by Sissy Spacek, as one of the young girls whose job it is to don a plain swimming suit, the uniform of the employees at the spa, and spend her day guiding old and infirm people safely around the therapeutic pool. She admires Millie, another girl working there and seeks her company and ultimately her identity.

Scenes of Desert Hot Springs' main street, Palm Drive, pop up throughout the movie as Pinky and Millie move around town. Pinky's first residence before she connives to move in with Millie, who has become her idol, was filmed in a room above the local drugstore. The druggist, John Furbee, who had recently purchased the building, remembers the film crew and how he was surprised they wanted to use the unattractive, poorly furnished rooms above his store. But the existing out-of-date furniture turned out to be perfect for the tone and atmosphere of the movie.

Other shots of Pinky and Millie driving around in Millie's yellow Ford Pinto are impossible to identify as any specific place since the background is mainly creosote bushes and sky and could be anywhere in the desert. A western-themed bar scene was located in Rancho Mirage at a time before major development transformed the sand and wind-swept dunes into upscale hotels and residences. Numerous views of the Purple Sage apartments were filmed in Palm Springs at a building which exists today, little changed from its 1977 exterior. An empty swimming pool with a painted mural on the bottom is a mystery location probably bulldozed and filled in some time ago.

Most interesting about the movie are Altman's own words: "We had almost no script, and made up the dialogue as we went along. Sissy Spacek was great in coming up with the right words for the scene, as was Shelly Duvall who played Millie. And then we also had some things happen that could have been mistakes – like when Shelly got into her car and closed the driver's door with a corner of her dress sticking out. Instead of reshooting, we left it and it made for a more interesting scene."

The movie was about identity transference and typical of Altman's genre, a dream-like, Bergmanesque drama. In spite of

Spacek's success with *Carrie,* the year before in 1976, *3 Women* did not click with the public. It was slow, difficult to grasp and very strange as Pinky slowly takes over Millie's identity while interacting vaguely with other dreamlike characters in the movie. However, it did provide experience for Spacek as she went on to become a major star. Among her later outstanding roles, many people remember her as Loretta Lynn in the 1980's production of *The Coal Miner's Daughter.*

While *3 Women* never made it as a popular movie, there are fans of Altman who are interested in all aspects of the movie. In 2009, the Desert Hot Springs Historical Society received an email from Australia. A fan of Altman's was inquiring about the whereabouts of filming locations in **3 Women.** He was making a trip to California and wanted to visit some of the memorable sites in the movie. He wrote, *"This brilliant film features some beautiful landscapes and buildings... Of particular interest is the apartment building used in the film called the Purple Sage Apartments...I would also love to pass some info on to other fans of this film, as the actual locations are a common topic of discussion on line."*

Whether Altman's movie pleased the general public or not made little difference to his loyal fans, those who understood and revered his work. Success or failure at the box office did not deter him from constantly experimenting with movie techniques. His career of ups and downs continued on through 2006 with a multitude of films, awards and successes, as well as failures. His unique and sensitive touch can be seen in pictures such as the TV production of **The Caine Mutiny Court Martial** or the movie theater productions of *Gosford Park* and *A Prairie Home Companion. Nashville,* (1975) was received as one of the decade's finest works and received five Oscar nominations. The Motion Picture Academy awarded him their Lifetime Achievement Oscar in 2006 to recognize his masterful career.

Mitchell Zuckoff, in his biography of Robert Altman, states that Altman was never entirely sober. If he wasn't drinking heavily, he was smoking dope or doing both at the same time. His goal seemed to be having a good time and creating a party atmosphere for the actors and crew. It was never important to follow a written script and actors were given great leeway to bring their own responses to the filming process. Perhaps it was this attitude that contributed to his genius and to his greatest failures.

For Desert Hot Springs residents, the success or failure of *3 Women* was a toss-up. While delighted with hosting a film crew and an admired director, expectations of a blockbuster movie ran high. When it was finished and residents could see the results, opinions were mixed. Weighing the thrill of seeing their town pictured on the screen, with sitting through over two hours of a slow movie with a difficult to grasp plot, brought heated discussions. Was it a movie to brag about? Perhaps with a few more loyal fans from Australia who understood Altman's genius, and if local residents could have seen merit in the work of this major film director, then more of the filming locations would be on the historical record today.

TRAGIC HAIRCUT
Janet Gaynor

When Janet Gaynor died in 1984, her doctor stated it was due to injuries sustained from an automobile accident two years earlier. But the details of the accident were never made public. Now over thirty years later, the true story of the car crash is finally revealed.

The sky in San Francisco was as clear as it gets on that fall day in 1982. The crisp scent of sea air from the bay blended with the smells of dry leaves swirling around light poles and food cooking in apartments. People were home from work and lights began to glow from lacey-curtained windows in Victorian buildings.

It was supposed to be a pleasant holiday outing on that Labor Day weekend. Mary Martin, known for her roles in *South Pacific* and *I Do, I Do* as well as *Peter Pan* had spent the day with producer, director, Paul Gregory, and his wife, Janet Gaynor, famous for her multitude of roles in silent films.

Martin had come to San Francisco to work with Hugh Downs on his popular T.V. program, The *Today Show.* Gaynor was a guest on the show while Martin served as hostess.

Paul Gregory and Janet Gaynor, after a summer on tour, were looking forward to returning to their home at Singing Tree Ranch near Desert Hot Springs in the Southern California desert. Gaynor had just finished a season of summer stock starring in a stage production of *On Golden Pond.* It was her first nationwide run of live theatre and the way things turned out, it would be her last.

When the phone rang that day, a year earlier at Singing Tree Ranch in the desert north of Palm Springs, Molly the housekeeper, answered. Gregory remembers Molly handing him the phone saying, "It's Miss Hepburn wants to speak to Janet."

Janet wasn't home and Gregory took the message which he later relayed to Janet. "Kate Hepburn called and she wants you to play the leading female role in a national summer stock tour of *On Golden Pond.* She really wants to do the part herself, but a conflict with her schedule doesn't allow it." Janet's response was immediate, "Let me read the script."

Katharine Hepburn was no stranger to Paul and Janet. She was a regular visitor to Singing Tree Ranch. Paul remembers her insatiable curiosity and her composure as two of her most charming attributes. In spite of her celebrity status, she had an "old shoe" feeling about her. And speaking of shoes, she loved wearing sandals and going barefoot. She often commented on how much she loved the feel of warm sand on her feet.

The part in *On Golden Pond* was perfect for Hepburn as she later proved in the movie version co-starring Henry Fonda. Jane Fonda, Henry's daughter, played the role of his daughter in the movie, which had to be an unusual and sometimes delicate situation.

As Janet considered whether or not to accept the part, she was concerned whether her small frame and gentle demeanor would work on live stage in portraying the strong, independent-minded, often crusty, elderly woman in the play.

The whole of Janet's career had been movies, fifty in all, in which her roles had generally been those of a warm, sympathetic woman, which worked with her small, petite, physical frame. As the first woman to receive an academy award, she had no doubts about her ability to portray a character, only whether she could adapt to live theater.

Gregory, Janet's husband and master of live stage production, had no doubts about her ability to conquer a role in front of a live audience. He convinced her that with his coaching she could do it. After all he had recognized Charles Laughton's talent and made his reputation by booking him all over the country to do readings on stage. If anyone knew what the audience of live theatre would respond to, it was Paul Gregory.

By this time he had already produced seventeen Broadway shows. *John Brown's Body* starring Tyrone Power and Judith Anderson and *The Caine Mutiny Court Martial* starring Henry Fonda and Lloyd Nolan were already stage classics.

On this fateful day in San Francisco, the tour of *On Golden Pond,* on what was known as the Straw Hat Circuit had come to a successful conclusion with Janet's outstanding performance in the role of the straight-spoken, sometimes even cantankerous female lead. Radiant with the aftermath of having added a new dimension to her career, Janet and Paul delayed leaving for their home in the desert. A weekend holiday in San Francisco with Mary Martin and her manager, Ben Washer, seemed like a good idea.

The four of them agreed on Grants Chinese Restaurant for dinner and hailed a Luxor taxi cab to take them to San Francisco's China Town. As the cab threaded its way through the narrow and congested streets of the City by the Bay, Paul sat in the front passenger's seat. Mary, Janet and Ben were in the back. The atmosphere was festive and Mary began talking to the cab driver, suggesting he would be far more handsome with a shorter haircut. The driver was flattered and responded to Mary's comments with a shy smile, saying, "Well, maybe when I get my next haircut."

"Why wait," said Mary, as she searched in her oversized shoulder bag for the small scissors she knew was tucked away in a side pocket. Leaning forward in her seat, she pulled on one of the cabbie's black curls and snipped it off. Then another and another.

The driver, surprised, but pleased with the attention, leaned over to view himself in the rear view mirror. He patted his newly shorn hair and turned his head from side to side to admire his new look.

Robert Cato, visiting from Denver, may have been unacquainted with the streets in San Francisco. He was driving a van and approaching from the right. He'd had way too many drinks and the world seemed a little fuzzy and out of focus to him. On the corner of California Street and Franklin, the red light signaling him to stop simply didn't register in his inebriated brain. As the taxi carrying four happy people to dinner entered the intersection, Robert Cato sped through the red light and crashed broadside into the moving cab. The force of the impact spun the taxi around three times before it careened to a stop.

Paul Gregory in the front seat saw Robert Cato coming and though he was able to brace himself for the crash, he still suffered three broken ribs and a number of lesser injuries. The cab driver emerged with a few scratches and minor bruises. Robert Cato, the drunken driver, was also relatively unhurt. Mary Martin in the back seat of the cab behind the driver was thrown out of the car and sustained some damage she was able to recover from. Her manager, Ben Washer, seated on the right behind Paul, took the brunt of the crash and was killed outright. Petite, small-boned Janet, sandwiched in the middle between Mary and Ben was simply crushed in the horrendous impact. With eleven broken ribs, a fractured collarbone, numerous pelvic fractures, a damaged kidney and injured bladder, she was in serious and precarious condition.

A few days after the accident when Mary Martin and her son, Larry, came to see Janet in her hospital room, she was still in a coma and Mary's attempts to have her picture taken with the seriously injured Janet were not allowed by Gregory who stayed by her side.

Over the next two years, life for Janet consisted of one operation after another in an attempt to repair her broken body. Complications often developed and she survived in a haze of pain and medication. When she died at Desert Regional Hospital in Palm Springs from pneumonia, she was back in her beloved desert, but unfortunately not in her beloved desert home at Singing Tree Ranch across the freeway in Desert Hot Springs.

Her doctor, Bart Apfelbaum, said, "The injuries she suffered in the 1982 accident two years ago really were the cause of her death. It was amazing she survived for as long as she did with the massive damage done to her body from the horrendous impact of the crash."

Janet was 73 at the time of the accident, Mary Martin was 68, Paul Gregory was 61 and Ben Washer had turned 76. The small scissors used for the driver's haircut was never recovered from the debris of the crash.

SECRETS
Joseph Wambaugh

Joseph Aloysius Wambaugh Jr. began his writing career with the publication of a novel, *The New Centurions,* in 1971. The book became an immediate success. His reputation as an author built with his next novel, *The Blue Knight* (1972). Next came *The Onion Field* (1973) a nonfiction book about policemen, and two years later, *The Choir Boys,* (1975).

Wambaugh wrote these books while still working in the detective division of the Los Angeles Police Department where he served from 1960 until 1974, first as an officer and finally as Detective Sergeant. He once commented, "I would have guys in handcuffs asking me for autographs." Finally, as his role as an author infringed more and more on his career in the police department, he resigned and turned to writing full time. In all he has fourteen fiction and five nonfiction books to his credit.

On a desert television station in 2010, Gloria Greer, a local reporter, conducted an interview with Wambaugh. It would have been interesting if Greer had asked him if his middle name, Aloysius, had any bearing on his own experiences. Certainly, it was a name that might need defending, whether from bullies in grade school or rival cops in the precincts. But, since Wambaugh says being a cop was the most fun he ever had, Aloysius as a middle name, may not have been a problem for him. Wambaugh also admitted to lacking computer skills. His novels were written on a typewriter with carbon copies.

One of Greer's questions was, "Of the three books you've

written involving the Coachella Valley, which is your favorite?"

Without hesitation he answered, *"The Secrets of Harry Bright."*

Gloria followed up with another question, "That book took place in Desert Hot Springs. Why did you choose that one?"

"It's because of the complexity of the characters," Wambaugh said.

He went on to explain that in his 1985 fiction novel, *The Secrets of Harry Bright,* the main characters had a variety of motivations and life experiences which added to the intricately woven plot of the story.

As events unfold, two Los Angeles detectives are asked by a wealthy Palm Springs resident to come to the desert and investigate the murder of his son. A burned out car containing his charred body has been discovered in a remote canyon north of Desert Hot Springs, renamed Mineral Springs in the book. With promises of money, time for golf and mixing with high society at exclusive country clubs in Palm Desert and Rancho Mirage, the detectives are willing to leave Los Angeles to investigate an event outside of their jurisdiction. As they collect information concerning the murder, they interact with officers in the Mineral Springs police department who have their own idiosyncrasies and secrets. Descriptions of local characters found in the desert town's watering hole add another dimension to the already colorful and sometimes bawdy story.

Those who read *The Secrets of Harry Bright* may have wondered if it was an authentic picture of life in the small desert town of Desert Hot Springs. Probably the majority of readers didn't care if it was true to the spirit of the desert or not. But in the 1980's, there were enough interesting personalities who lived in Desert Hot Springs to have inspired Wambaugh. Whether they were an exact fit for those portrayed in his book, wasn't an issue that concerned him. He could create a complex character from a few shards of personality. For example, in *Hollywood Moon,* (2009) a work of fiction, he used the true case of a rapist with strong ties to his mother as one of the stories tying together other anecdotes in the book.

His reputation as an author continued with *The Black Marble* (1978), *The Glitter Dome* (1981), *The Delta Star* (1983) and *Lines and Shadows* (1984) before *The Secrets of Harry Bright* hit the bookstores 1985.

In *The Secrets of Harry Bright* Wambaugh describes a popular small town tavern in Mineral Springs and the characters who frequent it. One of the residents of Desert Hot Springs recalls just such a place located on Indian Avenue. It was on the second floor of an A-frame building in what was then a trailer park. Everyone knew the bar as Three-Toed Pete's. Out of the way and tucked into an unlikely building, its clientele was safe from observation. Movie stars on their way to the high desert or just plain out slumming found it a comfortable stop, where everyone was accepted - no questions asked - no autograph hounds at work.

According to the current security guard, Clark Gable is said to have spent time there. Prior to the 1980's, the Triple L Ranch occupied the grounds. Some time later the name was changed to Two Springs Resort. The A-frame building housing the bar has since been incorporated into the office building in such a way that the only remnants of its original structure are two outwardly slanted supports that once would have continued upward to form the A shape. The red paint of the original building, has been covered over with a more contemporary soft beige desert color.

The building housing Rose Mortuary on Pierson Avenue just west of Palm Drive was at one time another of those hideaways where celebrities could show up and be treated the same as the great unwashed public. As the Lost Dutchman Tavern, it was a draw for popular movie stars who weren't interested in signing autographs. Steve McQueen and Ali McGraw were known to ride in on Steve's motorcycle and hang around till the wee hours.

The Lost Dutchman was also the unofficial headquarters for one of the most successful real estate salesmen in the area for many years. Along with selling the most property in and around Desert Hot Springs, he was also known for consuming the most alcohol. He could easily be a model for one of the locals described in Wambaugh's book. Wambaugh delighted in writing about this kind of person, accentuating both virtues and flaws.

Wambaugh and his wife, Dee, have a home on Newport Coast in Orange County and also maintain a vacation home in the Coachella Valley. As a part time desert resident, Wambaugh understands desert society better than many writers who are merely using the desert as an exotic setting.

Wambaugh, a prolific and popular writer of nineteen books between 1971 and 2009, brought a sense of recognition to Desert Hot Springs as a location in the same way, movie director Robert Altman, did when he used the town as the setting for his film, **3 Women.** Places gain celebrity status as well as people through noteworthy events or through their use as background. Details based on truth create a perception of place. They may be authentic or highly fictionalized, but the interest they create takes over either way.

Wambaugh's characters are drawn from life as are many of his stories. He does his research by treating small groups of policemen to dinner or drinks and encouraging them to talk about their experiences. Women, he says, are even better to interview than men because they are more willing to open up and discuss their feelings. Men are less likely to share and have to be prodded along.

Police dramas, real life crime and colorful characters are the basis of Wambaugh's stories. Some of his books were translated into feature films or TV-movies. *The Blue Knight* was made into an Emmy-winning 1973 TV miniseries starring

William Holden. James Woods starred in **The Onion Field** and **The Black Marble,** for which Wambaugh's screenplay won an Edgar Award from the Mystery Writers of America The movie adaptation for **The Choirboys** was the only one which did not go over with the public.

Whether the character of Harry Bright in **The Secrets of Harry Bright** was based on a real person, Wambaugh has never revealed, and Harry's secrets are not uncovered until the end of the book. Did Desert Hot Springs have a real Harry Bright? Wambaugh at his best placed a complex character in a setting equally diverse, which may explain why he chose **The Secrets of Harry Bright** as his favorite Coachella Valley novel.

From Sets to Submarines
Walter Cronkite, Natalie Wood

On his way to the CBS newsroom for his famous nightly news broadcasts, Walter Cronkite nearly always stopped at the set design bay. If the doors were open, he'd peer inside and call out, "Hey, Laws, where are we today?" Wesley Laws, a set decorator, would invite Cronkite in and show him the kitchen, hospital, living room or whatever stage set was being prepared for the current show he was working on. Cronkite always expressed interest and asked questions. He'd look around and then leave for his own show saying, "O.K. You take care."

One day when Laws was creating a woodland scene, Cronkite glanced in and said, "Where are we in the woods?" Laws escorted him around the set and explained how they were creating the crash scene of a small private plane. Laws explained how the airplane they rented had to have its wings removed in order to truck the fuselage through New York City streets. Once in the studio, they'd placed the plane at an angle in dense underbrush and reattached the wings with one askew. Cronkite was fascinated and walked around the set asking questions while examining the set. "This looks real. It must have been great fun putting this together," he said. He lingered for quite some time until a call came from his studio saying they were ready to broadcast the evening news show and Cronkite should get there right away. He began to hurry out, but then turned and came back. He shook Laws' hand, saying. "Good job, good job," as a frantic voice on the loudspeaker again urged him to the newsroom. He left and arrived on his own set with only seconds to spare.

Laws remembered the incident because it was so characteristic of Cronkite. He risked being late for his own newscast in order to pay a compliment to someone else. This was typical of the newscaster America loved and trusted. Walter Cronkite served as anchor of the CBS evening news from 1962 until 1981 and died in 2009 at age 92. He was considered the most trusted man in America.

Wesley Laws is one of those people who, with an amazing background resulting in four Emmys, could have lived anywhere. But he settled in Desert Hot Springs when he retired after living in New York and working at CBS in set design for his entire career.

Ironically, he got the job at CBS by mistake. After graduating from the New York School of Design in 1949, he went to apply for a temporary position redoing the office of a new CBS executive. But instead of going to the main office on Madison Avenue, he went to their warehouse district near the East River. While wandering in the hallways, looking for the office with the need for an overhaul, he came upon the set design area. Again by mistake, he was ushered into the head of set design and hastily interviewed by an executive who was preoccupied and constantly interrupted by telephone calls. Laws remembers sitting patiently and listening in awe to the part of the phone conversation he could hear. Comments like, "What do you mean the elephant didn't show up?" or "How could you lose the train tracks?" or "Can't you rent another lion?" seemed to be the gist of every call. Laws as a new graduate looking for a first job was overwhelmed. He answered the few questions he was asked between the intrusive phone conversations and was told to show up the next day for a two week trial period.

After his first week at CBS, he was called in to design a set for the *Vaughn Monroe Show*. He came up with appropriate backdrops for Monroe's hit songs, "**Racing With the Moon**" and "**Ghost Riders in the Sky**." It was due to the aid of a veteran set decorator who took him under his wing and showed him the ropes that he advanced so quickly. Within a year he was transferred to the main facility on Madison Avenue where he stayed for the rest of his career.

He was assigned to *Studio One*, which presented a different drama with each show. He functioned as their set decorator for seven years. One of the outstanding *Studio One* dramas was **Twelve Angry Men** which went on to become a movie and live stage play. Laws recalls it was in this drama they wanted to use the sound of a flushing toilet to indicate a man was coming out of a restroom. "It took forever and the approval of everyone up to several vice presidents to allow such an unheard of thing," Laws recalls. He was also involved in set design for movies, including *A View from the Bridge* (1962), but his main work was for CBS specials.

Laws' home in Desert Hot Springs reflects his career in television and the stars he worked with. A photo of Walter Matthau in a submarine is a favorite of his. "We actually went out to sea in a submarine to create this set," he says. "We got to experience the sensation of being in a small space underwater. The producer of the show had arranged for the actors, director and ten of us working on the set to meet in New London, Connecticut at the submarine base, where the Navy arranged for a run out into the Atlantic. For authenticity, the actors were to be in the same place in the real submarine as in the scenes they would play. They had to observe the coordination of the sailors when orders were given so they could replicate it on the set. We were allowed to take photographs, but all had to be coordinated with the Navy, so that our pictures never showed anything of importance on dials or instruments. This all took place in the early 1960's during the height of the Cold War and everyone was very careful.

"The skipper of the sub was interested and somewhat amused with our research on his boat. He asked me if I was interested in observing a dive. Needless to say, I accepted with enthusiasm. I followed him to the conning tower and as I watched, the bow of the sub began to submerge under the waves. As it went deeper and deeper, I kept backing up to get closer to the hatch. The skipper said, 'What's your rush? We have plenty of time. I wouldn't lead you astray.' I believed him although I was still uneasy being exposed on top while the sub was going underwater. Finally the skipper said, 'Go.' I rushed to the hatch, but found I wasn't as agile climbing down the ladder as he was. His shoes were fighting for the same rung as my hands. He had led me astray because he didn't realize I couldn't clamber down as fast as he could and consequently, water splashed over into the hatch before the cover was secure. Only one or two quarts, maybe, but the control room went berserk. 'Water in the boat, water in the boat,' the shout went out. Next came, 'Who did it?' A low murmur passed around. 'It was the guy from the studio. He was too slow.' I felt completely humiliated. Finally the skipper piped up and took the blame. He said it was his fault, he hadn't given me enough time. That quieted the furor. I found out later, the hubbub was all about the report that had to be filed whenever any amount of water entered the sub interior. Apparently it was not the kind of report the officers wanted to make. That day spent in New London getting the right feel of the sub was not only extremely helpful in aiding us to get the right ambiance in the set, it was also pretty damn exciting and fun."

But the most satisfying remembrances of Laws' life with CBS in New York are the four shiny gold Emmy statues lined up on a top shelf above the sofa in his office and the six framed Emmy nominations hanging on the wall.

The first nomination was in 1969-70 for the ***Epic Journey of***

Apollo 11 - first landing on the Moon. His first Emmy award was for ***Beacon Hill*** (1975), the second for ***Love of Life,*** a soap opera (1978-79) and the last two for another soap, ***Guiding Light*** in the 1980's. They are daily reminders his life had meaning and provided pleasure for a multitude of people.

The pleasure was often personal as well. When Natalie Wood was performing in ***Miracle at Potter's Farm*** for ***Studio One,*** Laws was standing by when the director began to scold Wood for just standing there when they began filming. "You're supposed to start the scene with action," he said.

Wood answered, "I can't. I'm supposed to stuff a chicken and I don't know how."

In frustration the director looked around and said, "Does anybody here know how to stuff a chicken?"

Laws stepped forward and said, "I do."

"Well, show her how," the director said.

"It's very simple." Laws explained. "You see this hole in the chicken? You take a handful of dressing from the bowl and put it in the hole in the chicken."

"Oh, I couldn't do that. I couldn't put my hand in the dressing."

"O.K. In that case use a spoon and spoon the dressing into the hole."

Wood grabbed Laws and kissed him on the cheek while saying over and over, "Oh, thank you, thank you so much, I can do that."

The frustrated director said, "If I can break up this love fest, I'd like to get on with the show."

Laws has never forgotten this simple incident with the talented actress and was especially shaken with the news of her tragic death by drowning in Isthmus Cove on Catalina

Island in November of 1981. She was on their yacht with her husband, Robert Wagner, and after an evening of drinking and quarreling, Wood apparently fell overboard and drowned. There were questions concerning her death, but the final conclusion of the Los Angeles coroner was accidental drowning. With seven to eight glasses of wine in her body and the heavy down jacket she was wearing, it was thought she was most likely unable to pull herself into the small dinghy after her fall overboard. Thirty years later, the inquiry was reopened due to new evidence The mysterious and tragic death of Natalie Wood continues to be investigated.

At one time, CBS decided to do a special show with Walter Cronkite discussing the news with the four heads of CBS's foreign offices. The producer wanted the set to look like Cronkite's library in his Manhattan home and Laws was asked to visit his home and recreate his library in the studio. Cronkite said, "There really isn't much to see, but go and look anyway. I'll set it up with my wife." When Laws got to Cronkite's home, he realized Cronkite was right. There wasn't much to see, just a room with books and papers, and a big conference table, nothing of visual interest. Cronkite's wife said, "Wes, I know you could do a better library for him. Why don't you just create one?" So that's what he did.

He designed a set with a beautiful antique desk, paintings on the walls, books, attractive light fixtures, a beautiful swivel desk chair and stylish seats for the four visiting correspondents. A backdrop scene of New York City was placed behind the fake window and an attractive woven carpet in front of the desk rounded out the set. When Cronkite saw it, he said, "I'll take it – everything in the room. I love it – the desk and all." He was as usual just expressing appreciation for the work of others. He never did make any changes to his own library.

Walter Cronkite served as anchor of the **CBS Evening News** from 1962 through 1981. When he passed away at age 92 in 2009 he was considered the most trusted man in America. He was characterized by the Los Angeles Times as the "voice of certainty and comfort through defining events of the 20th century."

Many years later when Laws was looking for a small carpet for a particular spot in his own living room, he shopped in the various warehouses he'd used over the years as sources for set decor. In one, the manager showed him numerous possibilities and finally pulled one from the bottom of the pile. It was the carpet Laws had used for the Cronkite library set. Laws didn't hesitate. He bought the carpet and has enjoyed having it in his living room ever since.

When asked how he came to Desert Hot Springs from New York, Laws tells about his good friend, Bill Harp who had a nice retreat in Sky Valley, a rural area directly east of Desert Hot Springs. Harp had moved from New York to Los Angeles to work on the *Carol Burnett Show* and was lured to the desert by the weather and abundant solitude. He purchased five acres complete with an attractive rustic stone house. Laws was living in Brooklyn at the time and Harp convinced him to visit the desert. Laws came and fell in love with the scenery and weather, bought his own five acres and proceeded to hire an architect to design a house, pool, patio and all the amenities. But when he sought a contractor to build it for him, none would consent to take the job because he was too far away to be available for all of the decisions that come up during construction. Laws was disappointed and discouraged.

Harp wasn't ready to give up and then talked Laws into looking for an existing house to buy until he would be around enough to supervise building one. Laws found a home in Desert Hot Springs located high in the foothills on the back side of Joshua Tree National Park. The magnificent view looked down over the Coachella Valley and westward to Mt. San Jacinto and Mt. San Gorgonio. He moved into his "temporary" home in the fall of 1988. However, after a few renovations and the addition of a pool, he was so happy with his interim housing, he decided to make it permanent.

His decor is classical and elegant, with gilded mirrors and picture frames. He has room for his collections of Etruscan black pottery dating from 900 to 600 B.C., his malachite collection and Egyptian artifacts, one from the Moon Goddess temple of the Queen of Sheba. Photos from his days at CBS, paintings and comfortable furniture give enormous appeal to his home. Walter Cronkite would have loved it.

As with so many talented people, Laws never stopped working even after retirement in the desert. He designed exhibits for the Edward Dean Museum in Cherry Valley, worked with the Wedgwood Society, Cabot's Pueblo Museum and served as a docent at the Palm Springs Art Museum for over twenty years. He didn't choose Desert Hot Springs to get away from the crowd as so many others have, he chose it because his new home had everything he'd wanted and the most magnificent view he could imagine. Instead of Manhattan's towering buildings, he was surrounded by majestic mountains. The sounds and smells and activity of the city were replaced with the serenity of wide vistas. For someone who'd spent his life and career in the big city, the change was enormous. From a career of designing sets for others, Laws now lives in the best set design of all, his own beautifully furnished home.

LIVING WITH NATURE
John Lautner

In the October 5, 2008 issue of the **Los Angeles Times Magazine,** a feature article showcased the renovation of the Chemosphere, a house in the Hollywood Hills of Los Angeles. Built in 1962, by the architect, John Lautner, whom the article called "one of the geniuses of California modernism," the mid-century modern dwelling had fallen on hard times. Since 1976 when its owner was stabbed to death by two robbers, it sat empty and forlorn, a round space capsule-like structure rising as if in the process of taking off from the wooded hills at its base. Angelenos are well acquainted with this landmark that became famous world wide after serving as a set in the big screen version of **Charlie's Angels.**

In Palm Springs another Lautner-designed home, the Elrod House built in 1968, is also easily recognized from the James Bond movie, **Diamonds Are Forever,** (1971) starring Sean Connery. But only a handful of people are aware of a motel Lautner designed and built for Lucien Hubbard in Desert Hot Springs. Hubbard was an early 20th Century movie producer, best known for **The Perils of Pauline** and **Wings** (1928), both silent movies. **Wings** was the first Oscar winner for Best Production and the only non-speaking picture to win the award until **The Artist** in 2012.

By the 1930's Hubbard had invested in large blocks of desert land north of Palm Springs in what was generally known as Seven Palms Valley. He was entranced with the area's serenity and beauty set off by views of high-peaked mountains in all directions. It was a place for relaxation and getting away from the

Hollywood crowd. As time passed, Hubbard began to think about putting some of his acreage to use. His choice of John Lautner as the architect to design a development on the southeast corner of what would later become the city of Desert Hot Springs took pioneer courage since Lautner was young and unknown. In 1947 when Lautner designed the Desert Hot Springs Motel, he had not yet been recognized for his genius in working with light, air, sun and freedom of space, but he did have good credentials.

After graduating with a degree in English from a college in Northern Michigan in 1933, he served a six year apprenticeship with Frank Lloyd Wright at Taliesin in Spring Green, Wisconsin where he was put in charge of two of Wright's projects. Lautner then struck out on his own with a move to Los Angeles. He set up his own practice while still collaborating with Wright. In 1947 when he was hired by Hubbard to design the Desert Hot Springs Motel, his only other major commission was the Carling House in Los Angeles.

Hubbard believed in Lautner, but he would never realize the full extent of his genius since most of Lautner's work was accomplished after Hubbard's death. However, it was with thanks to Hubbard that Lautner was introduced to the desert with his first commission in the Coachella Valley. It was not until twenty years later that he was hired to design the more famous Elrod House in Palm Springs.

Lautner's building designs throughout his life were devoted to connecting people and the spaces they inhabit to nature. The ways he achieved his goal are still innovative today and the four-unit Desert Hot Springs Motel he completed for Hubbard in 1947 fits beautifully into that category. It is a rare example of Lautner's early "Googie-style" commercial buildings.

Lautner did his homework before he began the plans for the motel. After receiving the commission from Hubbard, he came to Desert Hot Springs and stayed at a typical motel to check out the weather and how nature affected the area. He may have experienced some of the winds which are prevalent in the spring and fall since the design of the motel resembles a walled fortress shutting out heat, cold, wind and sand, yet providing a light-filled environment connected to nature.

The few people who drive by this building on the corner of Yerxa Road and San Antonio Street, often wonder about the unusual architecture with orange-colored I-beams jutting outward from the roof to support a concrete and redwood exterior. When it was under construction, locals actually speculated that it was some kind of secret government installation.

From the outside, it is impossible to imagine the spacious, airy, units, containing a bed and sitting area, kitchenette, bath, and private garden. Natural light from a row of clerestory windows floods the interior and flows into the secluded garden. Each individual unit is its own environment with no intrusion from exterior sources. This concept of combining an indoor and outdoor living space into a completely private unit was a huge innovation in the 1940's.

Across the street from the Desert Hot Springs Motel, a swimming pool under an Oriental-influenced roof seems slightly out of place with the rest of the neighborhood. Currently the pool building serves as a club house and community center for the nearby Hidden Springs Mobile Home Park. Few people know it was originally part of the Lautner design for a larger complex. Why the entire plan was never built is one of those mysteries lost in the files of the unknown.

Records do show that at some time after 1947, a development named Bubbling Well, advertised lots around the John Lautner-designed swimming pool. Faded drawings on water-stained paper found in a drawer at Cabot's Pueblo Museum show two pools side by side, one seventy feet long of "striking shape" according to the sales brochure, the other said to maintain a temperature in excess of 100 degrees for those persons desiring hot mineral baths. The water came from a well supplying an inexhaustible supply of naturally hot water. Of the ninety lots available, twenty were zoned for business and only one street, San Antonio, on which the Lautner building is located, could have multiple units. All other lots were designated single family. The sales literature stated:

"Bubbling Well lies in the untouched desert, nestling against a bulwark of low hills and facing the towering Mount San Jacinto and snow-capped San Gorgonio. The setting is one of primeval beauty and grandeur."

In spite of the elegant advertising brochure, whatever happened to the Bubbling Well tract remains a mystery. No other information at the beginning of the twenty-first century seems available to explain why the planned development never took place. The only reminder of it is the name of a nearby street, Bubbling Wells Road. An "s" has been added to the original Bubbling Well name. No doubt it was also the inspiration for the name of Bubbling Wells Ranch, a private home, located several blocks to the north.

Similar to the Los Angeles Chemosphere home built fifteen years after the Desert Hot Springs Motel, Lautner's building in the desert also fell upon hard times. One of its owners, uninterested in architecture, rented out the four units as apartment housing. It wasn't until a knowledgeable and forward thinking entrepreneur, Steve Lowe, entered the scene some fifty years later in the late 1990's that the genius of the Lautner Motel design was recognized. Lowe purchased the building and began renovations to return the motel to its former brilliance.

He furnished the units with authentic 1940's furniture, complete with free-standing wood cabinet reproductions of 1947 television sets. The screens at that time were a tiny six by eight inches. Lowe placed copies of Lucien Hubbard's movie, ***Wings***, in the rooms and guests could watch the movie on the vintage type televisions. To expand the experience even more, Lowe placed valuable books on architecture and John Lautner in every room. He assumed some would be stolen, but he was mistaken. Guests were respectful and none of the books ever disappeared.

Lowe had a sense of style, so that walking into a Lautner Motel room lifted the spirits and inspired tranquility. He also had connections and soon "The Lautner" as it was referred to, was discovered by architects and interested people from around the world as they began showing up at the motel. Charles Hollis Jones, the innovative designer of acrylic furniture in the 1960's, furnished one entire unit with his floating Lucite bed and see-through chairs and tables. The Lautner not only came back to life, it was reborn with the spirit of John Lautner inhabiting every aspect of the building and its furnishings.

In Los Angeles, the Chemosphere's new owner, an executive at Dreamworks, placed the renovation of his acquisition in the hands of Marmol Radziner, a firm with a reputation as the premier restorer of classic midcentury houses. Coincidentally, Marmol Radziner and Associates had strong connections with Desert Hot Springs. When the architecture group developed a true modular home prototype in 2005, they called it the Desert House and constructed their model in Desert Hot Springs less than a mile from the Lautner Motel.

The L-shaped 2,000 square foot demonstration house is installed on a foundation on-site and consists of four cubes, all factory-finished down to the windows, doors and cabinets. Of the five acre plot just east of Mt. View Road, Leo Marmol says, *"You have a very strong relationship with the entire valley.... You see the (San Gorgonio) pass: you see all the mountains; you feel the geology of that valley."* Marmol, like Lautner, concentrated on bringing the landscape inside and producing a "green" building.

The new Desert House built by the Marmol Radziner

Company focuses on energy efficiency and sustainability using recycled denim insulation, formaldehyde-free woods, high-insulation glass and other environmentally conscious materials.

While building green may be thought of as a new concept, it really began in Desert Hot Springs as early as the first homesteaders in the beginning of the Twentieth Century. At a time when typical home construction materials were not easily available in the desert, rocks, adobe, mud and straw were substituted and became the main building materials. A number of rock houses still exist in the city of Desert Hot Springs.

When Cabot Yerxa began work on his Pueblo-style home in the 1940's, he scavenged used wood, nails and glass from abandoned desert sites to fashion his green building. In that same decade John Lautner captured light and provided protection from harsh desert elements in his design of the Desert Hot Springs Motel.

Cabot's adobe, Marmol's Desert House and the Lautner Motel, if connected with lines on a map, would form an elongated triangle on the eastern edge of Desert Hot Springs. While seemingly individual with nothing in common and styles a world away from one another, they are linked by a most significant element, that of focusing on green desert living. Coming from widely divergent sources, all three are essentially prototypes, interpreting the desert in ways that take advantage of its assets and use them for comfortable living in a land that can be harsh and difficult if not understood.

Though the Bubbling Well development was never built out beyond one building, the Desert Hot Springs Motel, its promoters had the right idea. Over seventy years later, their words still ring true. It would be difficult to find a better way to describe the call of the desert then these words from their literature:

"The spell of the desert cannot be captured with words. You feel it in your heart or you do not. It comes when first you see

the vast expanse of sand and greasewood ringed with magic mountains – or it comes suddenly after many visits – or it comes not at all. This is your world or it is not.

For those to whom the desert calls, this can be promised – at Bubbling Well, its voice can be clearly heard, with not a jarring note. There, silent, welcoming, at once friendly and majestic your desert awaits you."

For those willing to embrace the desert's charms, architecture as an element is necessary for maximum integration with the landscape. Using nature to enhance daily living instead of fortifying against the elements is the key to comfortable desert living.

DREAM AND REALITY COME TOGETHER
Steve Lowe, Beat Hotel, William S. Burroughs

Every so often, something exceptional crops up and leads to a different view of how one sees relationships. Like a sled gliding downhill on ice, once the momentum begins, there's no way to stop it until its energy peters out. That was the spirit generated by Steve Lowe, an entrepreneur and intellectual who came to Desert Hot Springs in the year 2000.

Many of Lowe's achievements during his lifetime consisted of connections, one person linked to another leading to another. The artist and writer William S. Burroughs had a term for these links, he called them the "interzone," which he defined as "where dream and reality come together." Steve Lowe was responsible for bringing two "interzone" projects to Desert Hot Springs, the Lautner Motel and the Beat Hotel. Both provided a literary legacy unparalleled in the history of Desert Hot Springs.

Lowe's first project was the renovation and preservation of the Desert Hot Springs Motel designed by John Lautner. Lowe rescued the architectural gem and turned it into an interpretive and educational site and retreat – a brain and body spa, according to Lowe.

With the success of the Lautner Motel, its guest list representing a world wide clientèle, its inclusion on architecture tours and its recognition as an outstanding example of early Mid-Century Modern building, Lowe, barely stopped to catch his breath before embarking upon a new project. His creative and imaginative mind began planning a rebirth of the Beat Hotel originally located in Paris, France during the 1950's. It was torn down in 1963 and Lowe intended to revive its memory and relocate it in Desert Hot Springs.

While the idea of creating a California version of an historic 1950's Paris building may sound a bit far-fetched, it made complete sense to Lowe. It was not so much about the physical building as it was about the concept. It was about the people who gathered in Paris and became the defining names of the Beat Generation.

The history of the original Beat Hotel began in 1957 in the Paris Latin Quarter at 9 *Rue Git-le-Coeur.* There, in an undistinguished, seedy, anthill of a building, the artistic energy of the times not only flourished, but to a large extent defined the 50's era. Major players of the Beat Generation - William S. Burroughs, Allen Ginsberg, Gregory Corso, Lawrence Ferlinghetti, Brion Gysin and Harold Norse were all associated with the Beat Hotel. This core group represented important artistic experimentation.

When Lowe who admitted he never watched television or followed sports, talked about the Beat Hotel, names like Ginsberg, Burroughs and Corso popped out of his mouth and bounced around like ping pong balls. Lowe's innate sense of familiarity with the Beat Era stemmed partially from his relationship with Burroughs. He not only knew Burroughs, he was a friend and collaborator of the artist and writer who influenced musicians of the 50's and 60's and created the term, "heavy metal." Burroughs wrote and exhibited his art internationally and at various times lived in New York City, London, Tangier, Paris, Mexico City and Lawrence, Kansas, where he died in 1997 at the age of eighty-three. Although he was a prolific writer, he may be best known for his novel, **Naked Lunch.** As recently as 1996 his art was recognized by the Los Angeles County Museum of Art with a retrospective.

Allen Ginsberg's influence as a major poet of the Beat Generation began earlier and extended into the hippie era of the

1960's. He is remembered for his famous poetry readings and bringing controversial topics into the open.

But how do these facts relate to Lowe's Beat Hotel in Desert Hot Springs? The simple story was told by Brion Gysin in his novel, *The Last Museum,* written after the razing of the Paris Beat Hotel in 1963. The novel, published in 1986, is based on the original Beat Hotel. In Gysin's book, the hotel is moved to Southern California and is rebuilt in a small town in the desert about two hours from Los Angeles. The town is located on the San Andreas earthquake fault and underground hot mineral water is discovered there. It is impossible to know where Gysin got his idea for moving the hotel, but it is clear Desert Hot Springs meets all of his requirements.

Impressed with how closely Desert Hot Springs fit the site for the relocated Beat Hotel in Gysin's novel, Lowe began a search for a building that would become the new Beat Hotel. An ugly, boxy, rundown two-story structure on Hacienda Boulevard reminded him of the hotel in Tangier where Burroughs had written *Naked Lunch.* When he discovered it had been built in 1957, the same year as the Beat Hotel in Paris began to take shape as a literary center, he dared to believe it might be the one he was looking for. As more research revealed it had originally been named The Monte Carlo, a good French name in Tangier, but not one common to the desert, Lowe knew he had found the new Beat Hotel, the reincarnation of the original, as described in Gysin's book.

Lowe not only renovated the building, he filled the rooms with furniture of the fifties and original William Burroughs' art. There were no telephones or televisions. Each of the eight rooms along with its vintage furniture also held a vintage manual typewriter. Scattered around the pool were more typewriters on small stands. To those familiar with Burroughs, the typewriters were reminders of his habit of doing most of his writing in various hotel rooms where he said his creative spirit was unleashed.

Along with the other memorabilia, Lowe displayed a Burroughs adding machine invented by Burroughs' grandfather.

Money from the wealthy Midwestern Burroughs family had allowed William Burroughs to travel extensively and live by his own rules. After graduation from Harvard University where he studied literature and anthropology, he experimented with various lifestyles, frequently took drugs, was fascinated with the gangster world and generally appeared in public wearing a stylish business suit and fedora. The cutting edge of society was his turf and nonconformity his obsession.

Lowe had worked with Burroughs as a professional writer, friend, and art collaborator during a large portion of Burroughs' working life. At the Beat Hotel, Lowe used two ground floor rooms for a display of his own collection of Burroughs' art. Included was a library dedicated to the study of Burroughs' work and related Beat authors. This extraordinary rich and extensive assemblage drew followers from all over the literary world, while local people were generally unaware of its existence.

Similar to its Paris ancestor, The Beat Hotel in Desert Hot Springs became a gathering place and one-of-a kind destination for followers of the arts, both literary and visual. Lowe described it as a living museum catering to writers. He arranged gatherings, where current poets like Anne Waldman read their work, discussions took place over a glass of wine and small musical soirées were held in the early evenings. One of Lowe's exhibitions featured his extensive array of photographs of the Beats by Allen Ginsberg and Harold Chapman who lived at the Paris Beat Hotel for six years. *Smithsonian Magazine* recently recognized Ginsberg's photographs with a feature in its July 2010 issue. Lowe invited local people from the Coachella Valley whom he knew would be interested in the spirit of intellectualism taking place inside the stark white building on Hacienda Avenue.

Due to its unusual and dedicated emphasis, the hotel was

featured in *Vanity Fair, The New York Times, Travel and Leisure, Interior Design, The Los Angeles Times, Blackbook, Palm Springs Life* and *Western Interiors,* among others, many of which were European magazines. And yet, most residents of Desert Hot Springs were totally unaware of the Beat Hotel and the art and literary depths from which it was born and which it fostered. Lowe never put up a sign with the name, **Beat Hotel.** You either knew about it or you didn't. Many of those who came to stay, made their reservations from European countries and the eastern states of the U.S. along with Los Angeles and San Francisco scholars and academicians.

Lowe, who was always dreaming of the next step, continually expanded his plans as new connections brought about new opportunities. His enthusiasm brought him new friends and respect from the architectural and intellectual world. The Palm Springs Modern Committee recognized him with their highest preservation award during Modernism Week held every February.

And then the unthinkable happened. One afternoon in January of 2007 Lowe didn't feel well. His heart seemed to be racing in his chest. He knew something was very wrong. By the time he'd driven himself to the hospital across the freeway, his heart attack had done its damage. He died that afternoon.

The tragic passing of an inspiring visionary shocked the literary community. Events to celebrate his memory and extraordinary influence in the desert as well as around the world were organized. The first was held at the Moes' Bubbling Wells Ranch in Desert Hot Springs, a place Steve dearly loved and visited often. Another took place later on March 15, 2007 at the Annenberg Theater in the Palm Springs Art Museum. Anne Waldman did a reading dedicated to the memory of Steve Lowe and 500 copies of a commemorative book of poetry and testimonials were printed. One man's influence on the literary world was recognized, not for his own arts, but for the extraordinary ways in which he preserved the legacy of others.

As the shock of Lowe's early death spread throughout the community, questions arose as to what would happen to the Lautner Motel and Beat Hotel. Foremost in the minds of all who knew and loved Lowe was that his death was not only the loss of a man, but also the possible loss of an architectural gem and a reincarnated cultural destination as well. No one else possessed the knowledge and zeal to continue the existence and influence of these two landmarks.

The Lautner was more widely known and there was hope that someone in the architectural community would step forward to save it. Eventually it was purchased by a couple from Los Angeles who were in tune with the genius of John Lautner and planned to continue the restoration begun by Lowe. So the Desert Hot Springs Lautner Motel lives on.

The Beat Hotel was not so fortunate. Lowe's sister arrived and began quietly disposing of Lowe's prized possessions. The museum quality art at the Beat included a collaborative work of Robert Rauschenberg and Burroughs, signed books and manuscripts from authors of the Beat Generation as well as the ugly, bigger than life, Mugwump,* created by Burroughs in his book, **Naked Lunch**, and interpreted into a figure by David Cronenberg in the movie adaptation. The figure from the movie had been donated to Steve Lowe for the Beat Hotel by Burroughs' publicist who had purchased it from a Sotheby's Beat auction and stored it in Allen Ginsberg's New York City basement. After staying at the Beat Hotel, it became clear the Mugwump belonged with Lowe and his other Burroughs items.

Mugwump is a term relating to the Republicans who left the party in 1884 to support the Democatic candidacy of Grover Cleveland. It has come to mean some one who is neutral or undecided. It reappeared in the Harry Potter series where Albus Dumbledore is the supreme Mugwump of the International Confederation of Wizards.

But the Mugwump was no longer a welcome figure when the building was sold and stripped of its Beat Generation and Burroughs memorabilia. The literary and art emphasis disappeared along with the name even though it never did appear on the building's plain exterior. With Lowe's death, the tropical white exterior was repainted with a soft gray, removing any resemblance to a building in Tangier. Tourists still stay in the rooms, but the furniture no longer includes vintage typewriters and original prints. While the building still stands on the corner of Hacienda and Hidalgo Streets, the Beat Hotel no longer exists. In its place is the Dog Spa Resort & Wellness Center specifically created as a welcoming spa for pet owners and their pets. It even has its own celebrity, Brad Pitt, the owner's beloved dog, a pit bull mix.

However, the question remains, since the Beat Hotel was reincarnated once, is the demise of its second life permanent? Or will it, like the fabled Phoenix, rise once again from the ashes to be established in a new location where literary figures can meet and elevate artistic energy to a new high for another generation?

PLASTICS: PAST AND PRESENT
Charles Hollis Jones

It was the 1960's and Charles Hollis Jones was the sought after designer of the upper crust. Loretta Young, award winning film and television actress, was one of his best clients along with Lucille Ball, Dean Martin, Frank Sinatra, Johnny Carson and Sylvester Stallone. Commissions came to him from top interior designers, Paul Laszlo, Arthur Elrod, Hal Broderick, Steve Chase and John Woolf.

As an independent designer, Charles was known for his pioneering work with Lucite and acrylic. His designs were recognized as the some of the best during the Mid-Century Modernist period. His best-selling Wisteria chair (1968) was originally designed as a commission from playwright, Tennessee Williams. "He wanted to sit in it every morning, to start his day in it," Charles said. Williams purchased other items from Charles with the requirement that the designer have a drink with him.

It was in 1961 that Charles Hollis Jones' career began to take shape. He was sixteen years old and in love with glass as a creative material for furniture design. But glass simply wouldn't do what Jones wanted, so he turned to a similar but new material, plastic. Even though plastic had been around since the introduction of Lucite in 1936, and was utilized in World War II for aircraft canopies, nose cones and gunner turrets, its use in the manufacture of furniture, had been limited to the duplication of traditional designs.

Young Charles had a different vision and began developing

techniques to take advantage of the unique properties of plastic; it could be molded and cast into sheets, rods and tubes. By applying known techniques and some Charles invented using his own kitchen oven to heat the material and hand bend it, he was able to present a whole new concept in furniture design. His modern-themed projects emphasized the unique way plastic absorbs and reflects light, resulting in crystal clear tables, chairs, bed frames, lamps and decorative accessories.

The Hudson-Rissman showroom in Los Angeles known for "modern, high-end, good looking" furnishings in the 1960's carried Charles's accessories. But Charles wanted to do more. "I liked art you bumped into," he said, "not that you looked at on a shelf. I wanted to make big furniture. I wanted to make beds – they wouldn't let me put a bed in their showroom." In a bold move, opening his own showroom made it possible for him to expand his lines. Along with his highly sucessful accessories, (Frank Sinatra bought forty Lucite tissue boxes and an equal number of Lucite-lined wastepaper baskets), Charles was finally able to display his Lucite bed and other large furniture pieces.

Palm Springs in the 60's and 70's was a bastion of modernism in both architecture and furnishings. Charles' clean, crystal designs, as well as those in which he combined metal and acrylic were sought after by every high-end designer. They were especially popular in the desert with Arthur Elrod and the Palm Springs Movie Colony in the 1960's and 70's.

Then, as tastes changed and interest in Mediterranean style and classic extravagance began to take over, the clean lines of acrylic furniture lost their immediate appeal. In spite of the decline in commissions, Charles never gave up creating. But it wasn't until interest in Modernism revived that Charles' work was once again in the limelight. Modernism Week in Palm Springs brought him back to the desert and in 2001, he met a kindred spirit at the convention center where his vintage work was on display.

Steve Lowe had just finished renovating a motel in Desert Hot Springs designed by the innovative modern architect, John Lautner in 1947. While Lautner worked primarily in Los Angeles, he, too, had been lured to the desert by Arthur Elrod and had designed Elrod's house in Palm Springs, which stands today as an outstanding example of modern architecture. Many of the original furnishings were Charles Hollis Jones' creations.

In the Lautner Desert Hot Springs Motel, originally built as a retreat for Lucien Hubbard, the silent movie mogul and head of Paramount Pictures, Lautner had demonstrated his genius for combining sensitivity for nature with modern and innovative building materials. But just as Charles Hollis Jones' acrylic furniture languished after the decline of interest in Modernism, the motel also went through a period of neglect during a time when the clean lines of Modernism were considered passé and needed embellishment.

But Steve Lowe, a visionary, art lover and entrepreneur, saw the Lautner motel as a tarnished jewel ready to be restored it to its earlier luster. In order to find furnishings for the four motel units that would be as authentic as the building, Lowe searched thrift shops and resale stores. Ultimately each light-filled, airy suite was furnished with authentic furniture from the 1940's and 50's.

Consequently, when Charles and Lowe met they were each fascinated with the other's achievements. It didn't take long before they had forged a deal. Charles would furnish one whole suite in the Lautner motel with his acrylic modern furniture, including his floating bed lit from below. In exchange, Lowe would let Charles use the suite whenever he was in town. A bond of friendship was forged which proved advantageous for both.

Through Lowe, Charles became connected with Desert Hot Springs and more friendships followed. After he was invited to accompany Lowe to a Christmas Eve party at Bubbling Wells Ranch, a private home, another connection was made. Charles recognized three of his designer pieces in the home: a coffee table, vanity stool and mirror were all products of his once popular furniture lines. He offered to sign the pieces and on his next visit he brought his engraving tool and hand-signed the vintage items.

At this point in time, due to the resurgence of interest in modernism, Charles' work was again regaining recognition. His furniture made in the 50's and 60's was capturing and surpassing its original value. An auction, entitled "Innovators of Twentieth-Century Style" at Christie's in Los Angeles in 2000, brought good prices for eighty vintage pieces Charles had collected and put up for sale. A pair of spider occasional tables, favorites of Arthur Elrod, sold for $3,000. Two Metric Line lounge chairs and ottomans brought $5,500 and his Brilliance of Design Award Edison lamp brought $6,500.

In a similar way to the rediscovery and appreciation of the Lautner motel, Charles Hollis Jones' work was rediscovered and appreciated after some years of neglect and Charles began to spend more time in Desert Hot Springs with Lowe and his friends at Bubbling Wells Ranch.

But things change and disaster has a way of striking when least expected. With the tragic and sudden heart attack death of Steve Lowe in 2007, the Lautner motel went up for sale and not knowing what the future held for it, Charles removed his acrylic designer furniture. Without Lowe, who through his knowledge and constant enthusiasm brought people together, it seemed Charles' comfortable connection with Desert Hot Springs was at risk. However, as the Christmas season approached, the call came inviting him to the annual Christmas Eve party at Bubbling Wells Ranch. So he still had friends in Desert Hot Springs.

By this time Jones, once referred to by the Los Angeles Times, as a "pioneer in acrylic design," was more appropriately considered an icon in the field of acrylic furniture design. Frank Sinatra and Dean Martin had used his stools as perching places when they appeared on stage or television. The Smithsonian recognized him for his pioneering use of acrylic and lucite. Museums, including the Norton Simon in Los Angeles featured his innovative see-through designs. His client list included Johnny Carson, John Lautner, Paul Laszlo, Raymond Loewy and high end clients of contemporary designers. His furniture was installed at an exhibition in the Elrod House in Palm Springs in 2006.

Charles never rests on his past reputation. He continues to delight and surprise with new concepts and designs. His Obama chair has circles for arms. He twists and bends plastic resin into organic shapes with exceptional strength as he continues to move forward artistically. The February 2009 issue of **Palm Springs Life,** California's Prestige Magazine, ranks him as a "Master of Modernism" along with architects John Lautner and William Krisel as well as artist Karl Benjamin.

In time the Lautner motel was purchased by two young designers from Los Angeles with the intention of going ahead with Lowe's plans for developing the property the way Lautner had originally designed. Meanwhile, Charles continues to stay at the Bubbling Wells guest house when he comes to town for Modernism Week and while Steve Lowe is greatly missed, Charles still has connections in Desert Hot Springs.

Though Charles Hollis Jones' physical association with Desert Hot Springs as a retreat to a quieter more peaceful place didn't occur until the twenty-first century, his designer furniture preceded him by nearly forty years. His influence as a major contributor to the Modernism style of the 60's and 70's continues.

Time passes, but connections with friends and places of solitude continue to attract. The players may change, but the play goes on as the scenery and sets move from one site to another.

HIPPIE, YIPPIE, SATIRIST
Paul Krassner, Nancy Cain

When **People Magazine** labeled Paul Krassner, "father of the counter-culture movement in America," he immediately demanded a paternity test. Don Imus, radio talk show host, said, "...he is one of the comic geniuses of the 20th century." Krassner says Imus has since apologized for that quote, but that's just another example of Krassner's satirical and sometimes self deprecating humor. He calls himself an investigative satirist and his myriad writings and performances point out society's inconsistencies, but always with humor. In **The Realist** magazine he published from 1958 to 1974, he wrote, "The taboos have changed but irreverence is still our only sacred cow." He renewed **The Realist** in 1985 and presented it as an internet newsletter up until 2001.

It was also in 2001 he and his wife, Nancy Cain decided to move from Venice Beach on the outskirts of Los Angeles to the quiet, desert town of Desert Hot Springs.

The career of Paul Krassner can hardly be touched upon in a short summary, but he is distinctly known for a number of outstanding events. One was the anti-war protests at the 1968 Democratic Convention in Chicago. Many remember the Chicago Eight which included Paul Krassner, Abbie Hoffman and Jerry Rubin. Krassner, one of the main organizers, recalls how he tried to find a word to define the young activists who were against the war in Vietnam. He went through the alphabet trying to find a letter to replace the "h" in hippies, because the hippies were already politically radicalized around the world. He nearly gave up until he came to "y" and the word, yippies, was born. It came to stand for Youth International Party. A Chicago newspaper confirmed the choice with a headline, **"Yipes!" The Yippies Are Coming."**

According to Krassner, the purpose of the demonstrations was to "point out the ridiculousness of the actions of the establishment." His point became clear when national TV broadcast the roughing up of CBS reporters Mike Wallace and Dan Rather by helmeted cops. Even Walter Cronkite, America's most respected newsman at the time, called the police "a bunch of thugs."

Using satire and humor to point out hypocrisy in American culture has been Krassner's mission for his entire career. The direction his life took became clear when he was only six years old. A precocious violinist and the youngest at that time to perform a violin solo at the prestigious Carnegie Hall in New York City, he made the decision that would determine his life's path. As the strains of Vivaldi's Concerto in A minor played by Krassner, floated over the audience, his left leg developed an itch. Even at that young age, he knew he couldn't interrupt his playing to scratch his leg, but the itch grew more and more annoying until finally, he raised his right leg and used it to scratch the itch on his left. The serious and attentive audience burst into laughter.

That was the defining moment for young Krassner. He realized, he had the power to make people laugh. He suddenly knew he would rather entertain with laughter than music. Today he describes the experience by saying, "One person's logic is another person's humor. And that's still the filter through which I perceive reality. It's where my satire comes from."

Krassner went from that childhood epiphany to author nine books, record five comedy albums and write articles for ***Rolling Stone, Playboy, Mother Jones, The Nation,***

New York, NLY Press, National Lampoon, The Village Voice, San Francisco Examiner, Los Angeles Times **and** *L.A. Weekly.* He has appeared as a comedian on *Late Night with Conan O'Brien* and *Politically Incorrect* with Bill Maher.

The *New York Times* wrote, "He is an expert at ferreting out hypocrisy and absurdism from the more solemn crannies of American culture." The *Los Angeles Times* stated, "He has the uncanny ability to alter your perceptions permanently." From the *San Francisco Examiner,* "Krassner is absolutely compelling. He has lived on the edge so long he gets his mail delivered there."

For those who thrive on big city life, Krassner's permanent home in Desert Hot Springs could be viewed as the physical edge for a celebrity. Most of the residents of this small town have no idea of Krassner's international reputation, nor that he is actively working as a contributing member to his genre from his home in the desert. Nothing about his unimposing house stands out from the others on a quiet residential street tucked away from the main avenues in town. On many days, blood-red sunsets fill his western view with Technicolor so vivid they appear unreal. To the south raw desert spreads out and terminates in views of sharp-edged Mt. San Jacinto jutting into the deep abyss of sky above.

But Krassner as a person is as far from sharp-edged as one can get. Barely medium height with black hair tinged with gray that curls around his face like a fluffy halo, his dark eyes can't contain their laughter even when he's trying to be serious. He is gentle and soft spoken, kind and available. For some, his writings can lean too far towards the obscene, but the images he uses are meant to make a point rather than offend.

He's the type of person one would enjoy spending an evening with, except, perhaps, if you were an FBI agent. After attending one of his performances and in response to *Life Magazine's* favorable profile of him, the FBI sent a poison-pen letter to *Life's* editor, complaining: "To classify Krassner as a social rebel is far too cute, he's a nut, a raving, unconfined nut." George Carlin responded with, "The FBI was right, this man is dangerous and funny and **necessary**." Krassner takes it all in good humor and goes about his job of ferreting out the ridiculousness in society.

When asked how he acquired his pronounced limp, he explained it was the result of a beating from the police after the Moscone/Milk trial, (1978) in San Francisco. He had covered the trial as a reporter and jotted in his notes, "Twinkie defense." Afterward in his printed material he used the term again and it caught on. It is one more example of the absurdities Krassner points out. But when the verdict was announced and the "Twinkie defense" was legitimized, irate people massed outside the courthouse. The police came on strong, beating anyone within reach. Krassner, a bystander, was severely beaten and left with permanent injuries resulting in his limp. He says neglecting to sue the police department for his inflicted impairments is one of the few regrets he has in life.

When asked what he'd most like to be remembered for, without hesitation, Krassner says, "For putting out *The Realist*, a counter-culture magazine for adults. I had contributed to *Mad Magazine*, a counter-culture magazine for kids, but I wanted to speak to adults with satire and alternative journalism. One of my greatest satisfactions is having people tell me how *The Realist* changed their lives." In affirmation of Krassner's choice, a participant on a 2009 *Antiques Roadshow TV show*, showed up with a complete collection of Krassner's *Realist.* The collection was valued highly enough for it to be chosen as one of the items filmed for airing to the TV audience.

Paul Krassner, no doubt, had a hand in changing the lives of many with his non-conformist, humorous view of the world. On a personal basis, it is impossible not to like him. His wit is neither cutting nor aimed to hurt, only to to inspire thought. In between trips to Los Angeles and San Francisco for interviews and performances, he found time to fulfill a request from the producers of **Chicago 10,** to write the re-enactment scenes for the documentary which took place four decades earlier. His most recent award was a **Lifetime Achievement Award** presented in December of 2010 by the Oakland PEN, a chapter of PEN International, a literary organization.

In Desert Hot Springs where Krassner lives quietly, he occasionally focuses his satire on local issues. When the city of Desert Hot Springs was discussing going through bankruptcy, Krassner suggested their slogan, "Clearly Above the Rest" be changed to "Clearly Above the Credit Limit." When he sometimes attends the Chamber of Commerce breakfasts and introduces himself as "the local humorist" or with some other comical comment, many locals don't quite get it because they don't know his background.

They would be surprised to know that Krassner and his wife, Nancy, were guests of John Lennon at the opening of Yoko Ono's New York art show. Locals are unaware Krassner has been honored with an ACLU Uppie, (Upton Sinclair) Award for dedication to freedom of expression. And they never would guess that he took Groucho Marx on his first LSD trip.

During the years Paul Krassner was making an impact on the culture of the country, Nancy Cain, who would later become his wife, was working with a similar goal, but in a different medium. She was involved with **Guerrilla Television,** a new concept taking shape the same year, 1969, as the Woodstock Festival rocked and shocked the nation. It all began for Cain while she was working at CBS on a replacement program for the **Smothers Brothers Comedy Hour** which was being dropped.

"At that time, corporate dictated all programming in both news and entertainment," Cain said, "and there were no humans involved. (Cain didn't consider those in the corporate headquarters "human.") News events fed to the public were selectively edited with no thought of input from the public."

After Woodstock, a group called *Videofreex* circulated videos documenting the event. Cain said, "I'd never seen anything like it. While the big networks were only interested in the bands on stage, *Videofreex* filmed a document style program showing people getting up in the morning and the five mile long line of people waiting to use the porta potties. It was grainy and dark, but it was exciting and I knew it was important. I started using the same technique to do documentaries at CBS and they fired me. They said I was five years ahead of my time, but the truth was it was more like twenty."

It was then Cain became involved with the process she called "democratizing the media." While she and Paul Krassner would not meet until much later, they were both dedicated to the concept of "communicating without compromise," Krassner through satire printed in *The Realist,* and Cain with **VideoFreex**, doing documentaries around the country that concentrated not so much on an event, but on people interacting.

Cain said, "This had never been done before. Reality TV was unheard of and the public survived on spoon-fed selected news."

But Cain saw the future of news and video taping in a new way. She set off on her own with her video camera grinding away recording the real world. Ultimately, she became part of a cooperative that traveled around the country, showing people how to use video equipment and how to shoot their own local events. Then the cooperative hooked up the new people doing videos with their local cable stations so their documentaries could be aired.

"The cable stations didn't like it at all," Cain remembers, "but they had to do it because it was in their contract to provide community access. We felt like Johnny Appleseed," she said, "only instead of apple seeds, we were spreading community television across the country."

Cain's career took off in a new direction as she went on to shoot a documentary series which aired on PBS, publish short pieces, and as she put it, "open up the media to the people." When she reminisces about that period in her life, her passion rises to the surface and boils over.

The paths of Cain and Krassner finally crossed in Venice Beach, California where they lived across the sidewalk from each other. Drawn together through their mutual dedication to exposing hypocrisy, they married in 1988. In typical tongue in cheek fashion for both Krassner and Cain, the ceremony took place on April Fool's Day.

Cain would most like to be remembered for "democratizing the media." While we certainly have that today with cell phone cameras and internet access, Cain saw the possibilities early on and worked to get the ball rolling. She is proud of her part in that historic process.

Side by side with her husband, she continues her life's work from their home in Desert Hot Springs where few residents, if any, have a sense of how her dedication to the people's television has affected their lives. Celebrity status was never her goal, but making a difference always has been.

Krassner and Cain embrace the small town atmosphere and their careers from their comfortable desert location. Cain has a book out about her part in democratizing the media and Krassner continues his satire of society in a variey of works and media.

"That's Amazing"
Huell Howser

Along with the many celebrities who came to the sparsely inhabited area north of Palm Springs to hide out and enjoy some private time, there are others who showed up for different reasons. Huell Howser, popular California Public Television personality, was one of those who came not to hide out, but, instead, to help out. When he was invited to a fund raising event for Cabot's Pueblo Museum in 2002, he accepted without hesitation. Howser had found himself quite taken by the story of Cabot Yerxa, and the extraordinary structure he had built by hand from salvaged and scavenged materials.

He had already filmed the pueblo several years earlier and aired the episode on his own show, *California's Gold.* This weekly program consisted of a visit to an unusual or out-of-the-way spot where Howser interviewed people on site who could provide information. During these interviews, Howser was known for using the words, "That's amazing," numerous times. The phrase had become symbolic of Howser's remarkable ability to find interest in the smallest details others might overlook.

The fund raising event was held at Bubbling Wells Ranch, a private home located at the base of Miracle Hill where Cabot had originally homesteaded and discovered the miracle of hot and cold water reservoirs less than sixty feet from each other.

Howser had been invited as a celebrity guest to draw people to the event. At 6:00 P.M. Cabot's Museum supporters began to arrive, but Howser was not one of them. The party's hostess began to worry when another half hour went by with still no Huell Howser. She grew apprehensive and began to think maybe he was not going to show up. She hovered near the front door and check-in table for the 125 paying guests and wondered how she would explain his absence.

Finally, a tall, sun-bronzed, sturdily built man with a wide smile burst through the half-open double doors. The hostess exhaled in relief and stepped forward to welcome the honored celebrity guest. By the time she had taken several steps in his direction, ready to greet and present him to the waiting guests, he was already shaking the hand of the first person closest to the door. She waited, moved a step closer ready to say, "Welcome," as she introduced herself. But before she could catch his attention, he had already moved swiftly to another guest and was fully engaged in conversation. After several more attempts to unsuccessfully meet him face to face, she gave up and went out to the patio where the main part of the party was taking place.

It wasn't until considerably later in the evening when her path and that of Howser finally converged. It was then she was able to say, "I was a little worried when you weren't here at 6:00."

Howser, with a huge grin said, "I always come to an event after it is well under way because it's the best time for me to circulate."

And circulate he did. He managed to shake the hand of every person there and with great warmth and friendliness welcomed them to the event. Unlike many other celebrities who stand around and wait for people to come to them, he took his honored guest invitation seriously and he did his job well. One woman was heard to say, "I'm so excited. Huell Howser shook my hand. Now I feel as if I can't wash it."

Not only did Howser add to the spirit of the evening with his personal interaction with every individual there including the catering crew, but during the program part of the evening, he gave a touching and accurate account of the importance of Cabot's Pueblo Museum. No one could have been more compelling.

His performance at the fund raiser was typical of Howser. His popularity stems from the homespun and sincere manner in which he conducts interviews on his television shows. His intent is to show how everyone has a story to tell, whether it is relaying the history of a particular park, identifying shells on a remote beach or explaining the family business, which might be a small factory producing anything from custom tennis rackets to pizza sauce. Howser holds the microphone and conducts the interview like a conversation. He never does a trial run or uses any special effects or added lighting. He is always filled with sincere wonder and asks simple questions like, "How do you do this? How does this work? How long have you been in business?" His questions are invariably followed by his own comments, "That's amazing," and "Oh my gosh." Howser deals with the common folk and brings out their best.

He, too, is the best in what he does. Born Huell Burnley Howser in Tennessee in 1945, he began his career in Nashville. By 1981 he had moved to Los Angeles and worked as a features reporter for KNXT. After five years, he began producing his own local interest shows and series. Currently, he produces seven different series, of which five, *California's Gold, California's Green, Downtown, Road Trip* and *Visiting* are available free to California's PBS affiliates. He works without an agent or manager, has no makeup or wardrobe person, uses only a cameraman and editor. He can do a thirty minute show in the morning and have it ready to air in prime time that evening. After over twenty years away from his Tennessee beginnings, he has never lost his homey southern accent. It is part of what makes him so appealing.

Howser is quoted in an article by Robert Lloyd, television critic of the *Los Angeles Times* as saying, "Every single person we meet potentially has a great story to share." But perhaps the best story of all is Howser's own story. He's real. He actually does love talking to people. Maybe that's why he can shake the hand of every guest at an event and leave each one feeling important. He does think everyone is special, an attitude which bounces back and makes him special whether he realizes it or not. Robert Lloyd calls him "so old-fashioned as to be absolutely singular and therefore practically avant-garde." The world has always been fascinated by those a step ahead of their time and Huell Howser by being himself is ahead of us all.

Howser lives in Los Angeles and maintains an office there in the heart of the show business, television mecca. But he also has a home in the desert and spends time in both the upper and lower deserts. His success has not gone to his head. He is often seen around town casually dressed, just another friendly face. Yet he is also so much an individual, like no other that *The Simpsons* TV series parodied him with a character named Howell Huser. He laughs at the cartoon image of himself and might even be caught saying, "That's amazing!"

A Living Treasure
Paul Gregory

They know him at the hardware store, the Sidewinder Grill expects him for breakfast most mornings, definitely on Sunday, and the Capri Restaurant isn't surprised to see him arrive for dinner several times a week. In 2009 at the grand age of ninety years, he is internationally known, although most local residents in the Coachella Valley know very little about his reputation and achievements in live theater or much of anything about him other than he is a nice man. Paul Gregory doesn't seem to mind and is quite happy to be left alone to live out his life in the quiet neighborhood of Mission Lakes Country Club located just west of the City of Desert Hot Springs.

So who is Paul Gregory? If you are one of the people who remembers the 1955 movie, *The Night of the Hunter* starring Robert Mitchum and Shelley Winters you already know something about him, since he produced the movie and chose Charles Laughton to direct it. The story of murder and betrayal, but also of hope and good versus evil is that of a depression era preacher who preyed on the innocent. Robert Mitchum played the evil minister with the letters H, A, T, E tattooed on the knuckles of one hand and L, O, V, E on the other. Gregory said he selected the Davis Grubb novel as a movie project because "it touched me." There were parallels with Gregory's own life. He said, "My father disappeared after spending all of my mother's Indian money. He then became a roving preacher going from one small Mississippi town to another. Of course that experience had an influence on my interest in filming *The Night of the Hunter,* since that was the story of an itinerant preacher."

Gregory originally enlisted James Agee, writer and former film critic for *The Nation* to write the script. Agee refused to share anything about his manuscript until it was finished at which time it turned out to be a visual poem on the hardships of the depression. It was as big as a Los Angeles phone book and in its expanded version unsuitable for a movie. Laughton quickly rewrote the script with the help of two young UCLA graduates.

But it is, no doubt, due to the use of innovative filming techniques that *The Night of the Hunter* is listed in the Smithsonian's 100 best movies of all time. It was Laughton's first attempt at directing and his use of a brooding black and white atmosphere in the film is compelling. The movie is still shown in film classes and at universities as well as on television.

In an interview conducted by American Legends, Gregory revealed Lawrence Olivier was originally set to play the part of the evil preacher. But he was tied up with other projects for two years which was longer than Gregory could wait. He already had the financing from United Artists and needed to move ahead. So Mitchum was chosen for the part in spite of his reputation as a nonconformist, which included spending two months in jail for marijuana possession in the 1940's. He was considered one of Hollywood's first "bad boys" before Marlon Brando or James Dean. Gregory remembers the difficulties working with him. He said, "....people today want to hear Mitchum was a wonderful guy. Bob was awful. He'd be drunk. He'd urinate on the set. I had to hire a policeman to go by his house in the morning to make sure he was up and ready to go to work. Mitchum worried Charles to death. Laughton had to pull to get out of Mitchum what he got out of him." However, all of the hard work ended up creating a powerful movie.

After *The Night of the Hunter*, Gregory produced only one other movie, *The Naked and the Dead*, based on Norman Mailer's war novel. "I didn't like movies," Gregory said. "There's so much compromise. .....which is why there are so many so-so movies. And I didn't like the cutthroat people who make movies. In live theater, I dealt with more literate people. I went to Hollywood a gentleman and didn't want to wind up like the rest of them."

The Night of the Hunter wasn't Gregory's first relationship with Charles Laughton. Earlier he had heard Laughton on the *Ed Sullivan Show* reading from the Book of Daniel. He immediately recognized Laughton's talent. "Oh, my God," he remembers thinking, "I can sell this all over the country." And that was exactly what he did. He convinced Laughton to allow him to represent him and in a short time had arranged bookings throughout the United States. After these readings Laughton's reputation as a dramatic actor was made and so was Gregory's as a producer.

Gregory's main career was in theater productions that toured the country. He produced seventeen Broadway shows, five of which Laughton directed. Two notables are *John Brown's Body* with Tyrone Power and Judith Anderson and *The Caine Mutiny Court Martial* with Henry Fonda and Lloyd Nolan, which was nominated for a Pulitzer Prize. But when television began to show promise, Gregory moved into producing live dramas for TV.

From the outside Gregory's house looks like any of the other neat homes with well-manicured yards in the community of Mission Lakes Country Club. Inside, the living room is warm in feeling with cow skin rugs artfully placed on a white tile floor. Jungle-like potted plants reaching to the ceiling filter the sun's rays from the patio and bathe the home's interior with a soft glow. A basket of chocolates sits invitingly on a coffee table in front of the fireplace.

From the variety of major artworks on the walls, to Oriental lacquered screens, huge carved African sculptures, books and memorabilia, there is no doubt this is the home of a sophisticated person, one with a variety of interests and accomplishments. Awards and commendations given to Gregory by multiple organizations rest on shelves along with a wide range of interesting mementos. It is apparent everything displayed has a story and somehow figures in the rich and varied life of Paul Gregory. The white porcelain china pig featured on a fireplace shelf piques the imagination until Gregory explains it is a much-loved reminder of his years at Singing Tree Ranch when he was married to silent screen star Janet Gaynor. The pig held a prominent place on the ranch's kitchen counter. After Janet passed away, most of their shared possessions were lost in a fire, but somehow the pig survived.

Like the pig, some of Gregory's most interesting possessions are casually placed in surprising spots. A fine example of antique Della Robbia glazed ceramic ware hangs on a bedroom wall. It was once broken into three pie-shaped pieces, but salvaged and put back together by expert craftsmen at the Vatican without the use of glue. In another room a one of a kind mirror is framed with ancient carved wood demonstrating the finest of old world European craftsmanship.

It is on his bathroom wall that Gregory placed his signed Picasso drawing. It was given to him in Paris at a cafe where he was lunching with Charles Laughton and Elsa Lanchester. Laughton had pointed out a man seated a few tables away and said. "That's Picasso over there." Laughton waved at the artist and shortly, a waiter arrived with a note asking Laughton and his friends to join him at his table.

So Gregory got to meet Picasso and in short time, the famous artist pulled out paper and pen and within seconds, created a drawing, which he signed and presented to Gregory. "I can't claim Picasso as a friend," said Gregory. "I only met him that one time but the meeting was like so many others where I just happened to be in the same place as someone I admired.

"I met Warren Buffet in Omaha where he lived. I took traveling shows there and his wife was involved with the theater. So naturally at after theater events, I was introduced to her husband. And in the same way when my second wife, Kay, and I lived at the Springs in Palm Desert, there was a coffee shop I used to go to in the mornings because I'm an early riser and Kay didn't think it was morning until about ten o'clock. One day I got to talking to a young man there who told me about the house he was building at the Vintage. We had a pleasant conversation and when we parted and introduced ourselves, I discovered he was Bill Gates.

"Some celebrities I met at the salons Gertrude Stein held in Paris for artists. She was into haute cuisine. That's how I found out Modigliani was a drunk. He may have produced incredible art, but he was not someone I wanted to spend any time with. I met T.S. Elliot because he was fascinated with my Indian blood heritage and asked to be introduced to me. My mother was part Cherokee and I don't know why, but Elliot found that interesting.

"In Paris I also met Andre Gide and was introduced to Jean Cocteau by Charles Boyer. The crazy thing was, at the time, I didn't even know who these people were. Had I realized Gide was a giant in French literature and Cocteau, a novelist, playwright, poet, director, painter and heavily involved with the Avant-Garde movement, I would have been too intimidated to even say hello."

Just a few years ago, Lady Ann, a sister of one of England's Queen Mother's ladies in waiting, came to see Gregory. It was during the time when ten year memorials for Princess Diana were being held around the country and one was scheduled for Palm Springs. Lady Ann was visiting the U.S. and staying in Los Angeles when she asked to come out to the desert to see Paul Gregory. Reporters who followed her movements thought she was coming for the Diana memorials. But she informed them rather indignantly that she wasn't interested in that Diana thing, she just wanted to visit her friend, Paul Gregory.

Gregory had met her along with other royalty in London when he was teaching word dynamics at the London School of Economics. During his stage productions career, he presented **Don Juan in Hell** in the London theater, where the Royal Box always awaited England's royalty. Noel Coward, well-connected in England, made the introduction the night Gregory was invited to the Royal Box to meet the King and Queen of England.

Gregory makes it clear that in casual conversation he would never mention these incidents of chance meetings with very famous people. It was only because he was asked that he agreed to relate them. He doesn't like people who brag or try to make themselves important by whom they know.

In spite of Gregory's fatherless childhood, he was raised in culture rich London by his uncle. Because of hard times during the depression, his mother had sent him to England to live with relatives and it was there he was introduced to concerts, theater, ballet and all the cultural riches London had to offer.

When he returned to the U.S. for high school, he had a newspaper route which connected him to the local media. They loved his refined English accent and hired him to read the Sunday funnies on the local radio station. Thus began Paul Gregory's career in theater.

Ultimately he produced seventeen Broadway shows, five Charles Laughton U.S. tours, two first run movies and thirteen episodes of Ralph Edward's **This is Your Life** on television. He taught seminars in London and at San Diego State University. He was instrumental in presenting attractions produced by people from all over the world to seventy-seven cities. Name a major star of the forties through the sixties and Gregory most likely cast them in one of his productions. Some of the most famous were Charles Boyer, Agnes Moorehead, Dame Judith Anderson, Raymond Massey, Harry Belafonte, Marge and Gower Champion, Henry Fonda, Claudette Colbert, Joseph

Cotten, Ginger Rogers and Peter Graves.

There are stars he didn't cast, but nevertheless set on their career paths. "James Dean came to try out for a part in **The Caine Mutiny,**" Gregory said, "I knew he wasn't right for the role, but as soon as he walked across the stage, I was drawn to him. I knew he had something. So I told him to go across town to another theater and Elia Kazan saw it, too, and put him in his play. That set Dean on his way to stardom."

While Gregory is retired from the grueling professional life as a producer of theater, he never retired from coaching talented young people. Even in his eighties and nineties, he is still fascinated with young talent and finds it rewarding to teach them what he knows. He says, "Too many actors are not professionals, they have a gimmick. I'm interested in refining and fostering real talent."

It is not surprising Gregory works with young people. He's had a full life, created through hard work and seizing opportunity. He could just rest on his past accomplishments and enjoy the recognition that is constantly offered. But he is a sincere person who doesn't seek publicity. In fact, he shuns it. He chose the Desert Hot Springs area because he likes it, but it also enables him to live quietly and stay out of the limelight.

"Age," he says, "is a concept too small for me." And he's right. He is a big person, both physically and mentally. Smallness is simply not in his vocabulary.

THE END OR NOT

While I think of *Celebrities In Hiding* as completed, in reality, it will never be finished. Stories keep surfacing with information I wish I'd had earlier. However, ignoring newly revealed anecdotes just isn't possible, since preserving the historical record was one of my goals when writing *Celebrities In Hiding*. As new information surfaces even after the book is in print, I still feel an obligation to see that the material is preserved and available for future researchers. So, when Barbara Maron, from Cabot's Pueblo Museum brought me a set of photographs featuring Prince Franz Hohenlohe, even though the book was ready for publication, I felt it was important to see what I could find out about his connection with the north side of the freeway.

Paul Gregory, long time resident and international celebrity remembered the prince as a resident of Desert Hot Springs sometime during the 1980's and 90's. "He lived in a house just west of the corner of Palm Drive and 8th Street, near what is now Miracle Springs Resort and Spa." Gregory said. "I can picture the property. It had a tall hedge around it. Janet (Gaynor) knew him better than I did. I always had the sense he had difficulty with his role as a prince. He was born into royalty and raised in a royal family. Yet they were not sovereign. They had no authority, no property nor people to rule, so Franz always seemed somehow misplaced and not quite understanding of where he belonged in the scheme of things.

"I remember one incident when I went to Richard Waters's

art and framing shop on Palm Drive. I walked in carrying some prints I needed framed. When Richard appeared from the back room where he did his framing work, I began to explain why I was there. He interrupted and with a lowered voice said, 'We have to talk quietly, I'm handling royalty here.' Prince Hohenlohe was in the back room arranging for some pictures to be framed. This was the effect the prince had on people around him and it was something he didn't know how to deal with."

This small incident may be of little importance, but it confirms the presence of another person who wouldn't generally be thought of as a resident of Desert Hot Springs and therefore helps round out the historical record.

Another person of interest who needs inclusion in the book is the stone sculptor, Roger Hopkins. While his name may not be a household word, he is internationaly recognized. You may have seen him on the PBS shows, *Victory Garden* and *This Old House,* where he worked as a stone consultant during the 1980's and 90's. Or perhaps you've watched **Ancient Aliens,** or **Nova's Secrets of Lost Empires,** TLC's **Building the Impossible**, or the History Channel's **Mega Movers,** all featuring Hopkins' work. He is known for devising simple, but ingenious methods ancient people could have used to move monolithic stones, raise obelisks and build pyramids with only the crude tools available at that time.

Hopkins calls himself a "megalithic sculptor." His stone work takes place at his studio in Desert Hot Springs. From there the creations may end up anywhere in the world in spite of the fact they usually must be transported by heavy duty trucks and massive cranes. Hopkins work ends up in elite locations, including The Living Desert and Babe's at the River in Rancho Mirage as well as homes in distinctive developments such as The Vintage and The Reserve.

Hopkins looks upon stone as a primitive material with which

people automatically feel a deep-seated connection. He moved his studio from the east coast to the desert in 1999 because of the ancient black granite rock available from the local mountains. He says, "The granite here has a beautiful color and comes from deeper in the earth."

Hopkins' finished work may only be available to the wealthy, but viewing his work in progress is free for every car traveling on Dillon Road. At the stop sign and intersection of Little Morongo just west of Palm Drive, motorists can't miss the variety of massive stones standing on end in Hopkins' studio yard. Some have surfaces or designs polished to a gleaming black radiance. Others are stacked in henge-like ways that pique the imagination while summoning thoughts of remnants of ancient civilations. Viewing Hopkins' work in progress is a gift to every passing motorist.

Along with new stories cropping up, another problem that will no doubt occur is finding new information that adds to or even negates facts I've already put in the book. In one case, at least three people told me the same story and I felt confident it was accurate. However, at a later time, I was put in touch with a new source I hadn't known existed and it turned out the anecdote was very different from what I had written. In this case, the story had been repeated so many times, it was generally believed to be true even though its origin was muddy. It was a splendid example of "say it enough times and it becomes fact." Fortunately, that chapter was able to be corrected before the book went into print. But I have no doubt others of a similar type may turn up in the future.

Generally my sources for *Celebrities In Hiding* were from those who experienced the incident. If any part of the story is incorrect, it's due to the innocent, but faulty memory of those people I interviewed. I have tried to be as accurate as possible and in cases where detailed information was sketchy, the incident may be fleshed out with appropriate additions.

Another problem is that things change. History is not static. During the publication process of this book, the famous Capri Restaurant on the corner of Palm Drive and Buena Vista closed its doors. The restaurant moved to the Miracle Springs Hotel and Spa. The chef, a grandson of the Santucci family, was the only family member who moved to the new location to carry on the Santucci traditonal menu.

Celebrities In Hiding is neither a biography nor a complete account of any of the celebrities mentioned. It is a journey into the past through amusing stories that round out the historical record and may provide some surprises along the way.

Acknowledgements

Many people contributed information to this book. Some provided a number of stories, others had a few tidbits to offer. Together they are the basis for *Celebrities In Hiding*. Special thanks go to the members of my critique group: Gordon Gumpertz, Carol Mann, Gordon Davis and Carol Johansen, who advised me on on every chapter. Also Roberta Dinow who read the first version. Long time Desert Hot Springs residents, John Furbee, Delinda Angelo, Raye Horton and Jim Haidet were especially helpful. Dr. Richard Roger of Rancho Mirage contributed valuable information about the early days of the B-Bar-H Ranch and introduced me to Judge Jim Walsworth, Frank Sinatra's attorney. William Dailey gave me several good leads with fascinating information. Julia Santucci related incidents gleaned from her many years at the Capri Restaurant. I owe a huge debt to Paul Gregory for the hours he spent with me relating insider information about movie stars during the early years of stage and movie production. Listed in alphabetical order are many more who contributed whole chapters of information and interesting tidbits. I couldn't have done without a single one of them.

Frank Bogert, Nancy Cain, Tony Calsolaro, Mark Eads, Brian Edwards, Joe Farber, Ron Gilbert, Mark Green, Paul Krassner, Virginia Jacobsen, Charles Hollis Jones, Raye Horton, Wesley Laws, Inez Learnard, Steve Lowe, Barbara Maron, Daniel Plasse, Sylvia Rountree, Julia Santucci.

The Desert Hot Springs Historical Society provided a wealth of information from its archives of newspaper and magazine articles, letters and photographs as well as leads to follow. **Desert Hot Springs Why?** by L. W. Coffee was a valuable resource. Some information generally having to do with movie titles, stars and dates came from the internet. Ocasionally, I found it necessary to check with John Hunt's, The *Waters of Comfor*t for confirmation of a date or period of time.

For anyone who has stories to tell and wasn't contacted, I apologize. Somehow you remained outside of my reach. I beg you to write down your information and donate it to the Desert Hot Springs Historical Society where it will be not be lost to future researchers, but available when the next person is inspired to record history.